THE END OF JOBS

Money, Meaning and Freedom Without the 9-5

TAYLOR PEARSON

THE END OF JOBS

Money, Meaning and Freedom
Without the 9–5

ISBN 978-1-61961-335-5

Contents

DOWNLOAD THE BONUSES FREE!

Thanks for buying the book. To get access to all the free resources included (below), please visit **http://taylorpearson.me/eoj**

- Full Recorded Interviews with the Ten Entrepreneurs featured in *The End of Jobs* detailing how they launched their own successful businesses.
- 67 Business Books to Fuel Your Entrepreneurial Career.
- 49 Tools and Templates to use when launching and growing a business.
- A 90-Day goal setting worksheet to translate the book into actionable steps, and move you towards building an entrepreneurial career of freedom, meaning, and wealth.
- Access to a private community to discuss the book, and get support from a community of like-minded individuals to inspire, motivate, and assist each other.

Note*: Full names in the book refer to actual people. First names refer to real people whose identities have been obscured for privacy.*

INTRODUCTION

"It's only when the tide goes out that you learn who's been swimming naked."

– WARREN BUFFETT

"Hello sir, you want special massage?" A pretty Thai girl smiled as she framed the spa menu between slender arms.

A hundred feet ahead, wearing Croc flip flops, cargo shorts, and a San Miguel tank top, Dan Andrews didn't look like a typical multinational company CEO. Then again, no one at the Dubliner bar table fit the bill. I had just started working with Dan to manage the online marketing for a portfolio of eCommerce stores he owned with his business partner, Ian.

Next to him was Travis Jamison. 6′4″, a former bodybuilder in a white v-neck and fitted jeans with brown leather Oxfords,

Travis ran two multinational businesses—one manufacturing supplements, and the other selling online marketing services.

The trio was completed by an American woman. Curly haired with a bright Balinese skirt, whiskey in hand, head cocked back in a laugh, Elisa Doucette ran a content editing business for writers and authors.

They all turned to me as I approached the table. "Welcome to Asia," Dan nodded.

"Thanks," I replied gratefully.

The waitress walked up to the table, "You want drink?"

"Whiskey."

As she turned to leave, Dan informed me: "We were just talking about the conference this weekend. We've sold out. There are going to be *seventy-five* entrepreneurs coming."

The way he said it, you would have thought he was announcing U.S. gold medalists. A *whole* seventy-five people at a business conference.

It was by far the smallest business conference I'd ever heard of.

As the night wore on, more conference attendees trickled into the Irish pub.

There was Jimmy who, with his partner Doug, was working to

start a company selling travel gear. The pair of Kiwis had met at an exchange program in Canada and, over a North American road trip, agreed to alternate short-term stints at jobs and living off of savings, working to launch their company. At the time Doug was still at his job in New Zealand and Jimmy was fresh off the plane from the Philippines where he had been working on sourcing moisture wicking, wrinkle-resistant dress shirts.

Jesse Lawler, who had spent his twenties living in Los Angeles directing independent films, had given up trying to raise money for movies, taught himself to code, and started doing freelance software development building iPhone Apps a year earlier.

Dan Norris had a year's worth of savings from selling his web design company, and was in the process of building a software startup, Informly, designed as an all-in-one dashboard for online businesses.

What was going on? I'd read popular books like *The 4-Hour Workweek* about entrepreneurship. I even had some friends freelancing or running small companies. But I didn't quite *get it.*

Two years later, in 2014, the small conference had grown by 400%, from seventy-five to three hundred entrepreneurs.

I had been managing a couple of Dan and Ian's businesses. I had grown the eCommerce business, which sold fold up, portable bars to caterers and hotels, by 527% over the same two-year period that wages for jobs in the U.S. were growing 0.5% per year.

Jimmy was back, and Doug had quit his job in New Zealand. The travel shirt idea had been put on hold—getting shirts custom tailored in the Philippines is easier said than done. Instead, they had raised $341,393 through a Kickstarter campaign for their Minaal travel backpack at the end of 2013 in just thirty days, so they'd shifted focus to the faster growing product line.

Jesse Lawler was back. His freelance software development had grown from a one-man show into a software development agency for iPhone Apps, run from his house in Vietnam. In between drinking coconuts, he was funneling the profits from his agency into building his own product suite and hosting a podcast about smart drugs used for cognitive enhancement.

Dan Norris was back. He had spent nine months and nearly his entire savings trying to build Informly. Two weeks before he needed to get a job to support his family in Australia, he had launched WP Curve, an outsourced service for software development, on pace to do over a million dollars in revenue in 2015.

It's hard to square these two-year stories with the stories of my friends from college over the same period.

Back in Columbus, Max had graduated with me and was working at one of the bigger accounting firms in town. He was anxious in the wake of his two-year performance review. He'd placed third out of five in his department despite working fifty- and sixty-hour weeks in the months leading up to tax time in April. He felt grateful for the 3% cost of living raise he'd gotten each year. His girlfriend's parents were proud. He was "putting in his time."

Julian had gotten into one of the nation's top law schools. He'd done well and, as a result, had already gotten a position with a top San Francisco law firm. Like most people starting a career in law, he was planning to spend the next three to five years working long hours, sometimes eighty- to one-hundred-hour weeks at the firm, to build a reputation and pay off his student loans. He eventually wanted to start a family and hoped to move to a smaller, more affordable city where he could take a position with better work-life balance.

Marie had gotten into medical school straight out of college and was in the process of choosing her specialty. She'd always wanted to be a family practitioner, but Medicare and insurance reimbursements for primary care doctors like family medicine and internists had dropped so low, she feared there was no way she could pay back the loans and make a decent living. Instead, she'd opted for Anesthesiology, fingers-crossed that reimbursements wouldn't continue to fall for specialist physicians.

What was going on? What's the difference between my friends from college and the three hundred entrepreneurs now emigrating to Bangkok in flip flops?

From the outside looking in, both groups were intelligent and hard working. Why was one group living in fear of the threat of job loss, unreasonably long hours, and shrinking wages, while another was so overwhelmed by new opportunities they don't know what to do?

Two years after I'd first shown up in Bangkok, I finally got it.

WHAT'S YOUR SECRET?

> *"If you do things that are safe but feel risky, you gain a significant advantage in the marketplace."*
>
> – SETH GODIN

Multi-millionaire investor Peter Thiel begins every interview with companies he's considering investing in with the same three questions:

What's your secret?

What important truth do very few people agree with you on?

What do you believe that is both contrarian and correct?

What Thiel and the group in Bangkok understood is based on an old axiom from Archimedes over two thousand years ago: "Give me a lever long enough and a fulcrum on which to place it, and I shall move the world."

Any system, be it a mechanical one with a literal lever and fulcrum or a more complex one like your career and life, has leverage points. Despite pushing just as hard, sometimes your work is rewarded greatly, and sometimes not.

What separated my college friends from the entrepreneurs I was hanging out with?

Turns out, not that much. Both groups were ambitious, smart, and pushing hard.

After interviewing, speaking with, and working with hundreds of people on both sides, the difference then became clear:

The secret—a more strategically placed lever and fulcrum.

THE NEW LEVERAGE POINT

The rapid development of technology and globalization has changed the leverage points in accumulating wealth: money, meaning and freedom.

The social and technological inventions of the past one hundred years have brought us to the "End of Jobs" while making entrepreneurship safer, more accessible, and more profitable than ever.

Globalization is not just continuing—it's accelerating. In 2020 there will be 40% more 25–34 year olds with higher education degrees from Argentina, Brazil, China, India, Indonesia, Russia, Saudi Arabia, and South Africa than in all OECD countries (a group of 34 countries primarily in Western Europe and North America).

Not only have education standards improved, but the communication technology to reach and work with people around the world has improved in lockstep. Two decades ago, trying to call someone on another continent involved prepaid phone cards in cramped telephone booths. Hardly the way to run a company or manage a team.

Today, a $40 internet connection and a free Skype account gives anyone access to the greatest talent pool in history. Instead of competing against the labor pool of a few hundred thousand or a few million people in the area near you for your job, you're competing against seven billion people around the *world*.

The same technologies, machines, and globalization that have increased your competition in the job market have been a boon to entrepreneurs. They've dropped startup costs, opened new markets, and created new distribution channels. It's easier and cheaper than ever to make something and tell people about it.

For much of the past two hundred years, the industrial work in demand for economic advancement wasn't necessarily the work people wanted to do. Working in a factory may have been better than starving in a field, but it wasn't exactly a path to fulfillment.

After all, at the beginning of the twentieth century, college was considered a risky proposition. Why invest four years in a fancy degree instead of going straight to work? Just as college and graduate school emerged over the course of the twentieth century as a clear path to a job, life paths and social scripts for entrepreneurship are emerging that make the path clearer.

The opportunity to align your fundamental drives for freedom and meaning with profitable work is greater than you may believe. The stories in this book show that entrepreneurship is a path to not just more freedom and more meaning, but also more money.

Alas, there is plenty of work involved.

Psychologically challenging, emotionally testing, and physically exhausting work? Sometimes.

Worth it? Among the entrepreneurs I've talked to—*almost universally*.

This book will show you what those trends are, the new leverage points that define them—and how you can begin to use them to create more money, meaning, and freedom in your life, and the lives of those you love.

Whether you choose to fight the changes or embrace them is up to you. The opportunity won't last forever.

SECTION I

Have We Reached The End of Jobs?

"I am humbled to be standing here with today's other honorary degree recipients. William Schabas, human rights champion...is here to investigate Northwestern for cruelly allowing you to graduate into this job market."

– STEPHEN COLBERT, COMMENCEMENT ADDRESS TO NORTHWESTERN UNIVERSITY, 2011

In 2011, my Youtube playlist shuffled to Stephen Colbert's recent Commencement Address at Northwestern University during one of the worst job markets in the past few decades.

I glanced up from my notebook, a crinkled smirk on the right side of my face.

I had just joined the ranks of a rapidly growing class of people in the West: College-educated and unemployed. I was, relatively speaking, quite fortunate. Unlike many unemployed Americans, I just had to avoid pissing off my parents so much that they kicked me out or stopped buying my groceries and gas.

Anyone that's watched a TED talk, or read an article about the current state and future of science and technology, can't help but be inspired and excited. Never before have we had so much opportunity, and yet never have we felt so powerless to grasp it.

I couldn't help but think of the curse:

May you live in interesting times.

We certainly do.

Depending on who you listen to, between 5.1 and 7 trillion dollars in wealth evaporated by the end of 2008—the most ever in a single quarter.[1] Protesters camped out in lower Manhattan asking why the federal government wasn't imprisoning Wall Street bankers. While many viewed this as an isolated event, it is in fact one notable in a much longer trend.

Yet, as Steve Jobs notes:

> *"Everything around you that you call life was made up by people that were no smarter than you and you can change it, you can influence it, you can build your own things that other people can use.*
>
> *Once you learn that, you'll never be the same again."* [2]

The ability individuals have right now to deliberately design their lives and realities is greater than at any time in history.

I didn't believe it.

I always walked away from meetings with entrepreneurs and friends thinking, "They are really not any smarter than me."

Often times they were more experienced, but when they broke down what it took to build their companies, it wasn't anything that I felt incapable of.

The chair you're sitting in? You could probably design a better chair than that. Despite zero experience in product design or manufacturing, that's what Jimmy and Doug from Minaal did.

This book you're reading? You could write a better book. James Altucher, a writer and entrepreneur, self-published his book, *Choose Yourself*, that sold tens of thousands of copies. Twenty years ago, no one had ever sold that many books without being published by a major publishing house.

That class you're taking? You could make a better online course. If you're an environmental consultant, you could make the course for how to get hired by the best environmental consultancy in the area. If you're a nutritionist, you could make the course on how to do a 30-day program to retrain your habits around eating healthy food.

If there was a better chance to be successful (on better terms) out there waiting for me, why wasn't someone investigating my school for cruelly allowing me to graduate into this job market?

WHAT ARE JOBS AND ENTREPRENEURSHIP?

We hear the word "job" and imagine that someone is squirreled away in a cubicle, mindlessly filling out TPS reports for Proctor and Gamble.

We hear the word "entrepreneur" and imagine Mark Zuckerberg or Steve Jobs or Bill Gates.

Those are all true characterizations, but these two concepts leave a wide berth in between.

How do we clearly distinguish between "jobs" and "entrepreneurship?"

In his book, *Linchpin: Are You Indispensable?*, Seth Godin defines a linchpin as:

> "[A]*n individual who can walk into chaos and create order, someone who can invent, connect, create and make things happen."*

Allow me to borrow his definition and simplify a bit:

> Entrepreneurship is *connecting, creating, and inventing systems—be they businesses, people, ideas, or processes.*
>
> A job is *the act of following the operating system someone else created.*

Entrepreneurs may or may not own equity in a company. Peter Drucker, arguably the most well known management consultant of the twentieth century, was an entrepreneur in every sense of the definition above, despite not owning a majority stake in a large company.

The CEO of a company that is entirely accountable to a board or group of owners and mindlessly follows their directions is not an entrepreneur. He may call himself an entrepreneur, but he has a job.

I've spoken with plenty of people on someone's payroll who are already entrepreneurial and becoming more so—a process we'll talk about later on in section two.

ARE WE AT PEAK JOBS?

As a society, we've hit peak jobs. The era of largely abundant, high-paying jobs that characterized the second half of the twentieth century is gone.

Since 1983, the only segment of "jobs" to show significant growth were "Non-Routine Cognitive Jobs." In other words: creating systems.

According to a 2015 report from Kleiner Perkins Caufield & Byers based on data from the US Census Bureau, from 1948–2000, jobs grew 1.7× faster than population. Since 2000, the population has grown 2.4× faster than jobs.[3]

The problem both for us as a society and as individuals is that we're asking the wrong question: "How do I get a job doing that?"

What if the better question is: "How do I *create* a job doing that?"

What if job creation—something typically only spoken about by politicians or CEOs of large corporations—is something you, reading this book, can now do?

There are three primary reasons to believe that we are at peak jobs and approaching the End of Jobs:

1. Sharp rises in communication technology and improved global educational standards over the past decade means that companies can hire anyone, anywhere. Jobs are increasingly moving to Asia, South America, and Eastern Europe.

2. The notion of machines, both hardware and software, taking over blue collar factory jobs is now largely accepted—but now they're increasingly taking over white collar, knowledge-based jobs as well.

3. Traditional university degrees—bachelor's, master's, and PhDs—have become abundant, making them less valuable than ever.

Together, these shifts have all ended in a situation exemplified by an Atlanta-based law firm which requires everyone on staff, even the file clerk, to have a college degree because "it's a buyer's market for employers."

An article in *The New York Times* tells the story of Landon Crider, 24, who now works as the firm's runner despite getting his degree from Georgia State; and Megan Parker, the firm's receptionist, who earns $37,000 a year—which she is using to pay off $100,000 in student debt.[4]

Landon's and Megan's stories aren't anomalies—they're early

indicators of a trend that will have a profound impact on the next twenty years of your career.

Let's take a look at whether these assumptions are true, and if they are, what it takes to join the section of the Middle Class—not just surviving, but profiting from them.

First stop, Asia.

CHAPTER 1

LESSONS ON GLOBALIZATION FROM AN EVIL GENIUS

ON A RECENT TRIP I VISITED WITH NA, AN EXECUTIVE assistant working at an American-owned, technology company headquartered in Vietnam. Her resume was impressive. She was trilingual (Japanese, English, and Vietnamese), having worked as an executive assistant to the president of a large Japanese car manufacturing company. She was motivated and driven, frequently working sixty to seventy hours a week to accomplish the ambitious goals she had set for herself.

She lived in Ho Chi Minh City, Vietnam. Her salary was only around $1,000/month.

I've worked with computer programmers and designers based in the Philippines. They were all highly capable at both frontend and backend web development, and were talented in design and fluent in English. Starting salaries for this position would be in the $82,000 per year range in the U.S.

A typical starting salary for someone with her qualifications in the Philippines is often around just $700–$1,400 per month, with *exceptionally* talented developers earning around double or triple that.[5]

This isn't confined to just one country or region. India is now producing almost one million new IT graduates a year and more than a million engineering graduates.[6] Contrast that with the UK, which struggles to release fifty thousand engineering graduates each year.[7]

India and China are rapidly catching up with the West in highly technical fields: pharmaceuticals, biotech, electrical, and mechanical engineering.

According to an OECD report published in 2012, the United States and European Union countries will, by 2020, only account for around 25% of college-educated people in the world.[8]

Global education standards and the number of college-educated graduates around the world are growing dramatically.

Now, consider the initial wave of outsourcing that hit the United States in the early 1980s, just around the time wages stopped growing at the 2.2% rate they'd sustained for all of the 20th century in the preceding eighty years.

When you think of globalization and outsourcing, you probably think of blue-collar factory workers that have had their role moved to a factory in China.

Until 2001, that was largely the case. But, when another recession hit the U.S. in 2001, outsourcing accelerated yet again. This acceleration, however, was different than the one that had come in the 1980s.

Because of these improving global education standards and communication technologies, many of the jobs being outsourced were not blue-collar, manual labor jobs, but so-called white-collar jobs. They were jobs in information technology, such as computer systems analysts and software engineers, or were what could be called "IT-enabled" jobs (e.g. telemarketers and bookkeepers).

Any job that could be done purely over the Internet, even ones that required advanced degrees, began moving overseas in 2001. Since then, the trend isn't just continuing—it's speeding up.

GLOBALIZATION VS. INNOVATION: HYATT HIJACKING

Shan Zhai is a Chinese term used to describe the culture and practice of producing fake and imitation products, services, and brands.

Michael Zakkour, an American living in China, relates his experience with *Shan Zhai* after he stayed at the "Hiyatt

Hotel" on a trip to Dongguan, an industrial city in the Guangdong Province.

An accidental booking, his time at the Hiyatt revealed that a Chinese company had stolen the name (adding an i) and the brand experience created by Hyatt over decades at a cost of hundreds of millions of dollars was copied by China a few years at a fraction of the cost.

According to China lawyer Dan Harris: "[C]opying has only increased as interaction between foreign and Chinese companies increases." [9]

Think of how quickly seemingly identical products appear on the market now after a new product is launched. Things that seem obvious in retrospect, like putting wheels on suitcases, took decades to create but are now commonplace and quickly replicated.[10]

We have a tendency to underestimate how hard it is to do something for the first time compared to implementing something that already has an established roadmap.

It's much easier to globalize a technology, spreading it to another area, than it is to innovate and create one from scratch.

A new product that takes Nike years of product development to create can be copied and reproduced at a tenth of the cost within weeks by knock-off manufacturers. I've talked to people in China that have seen it happen.

The technologies that we now take for granted were incredibly difficult to develop the first go around.

Before the 20th century, the discipline of management, managing people, as we understand it today, was non-existent.

The father of management, Frederick Winslow Taylor, was credited by later famed management consultant Peter Drucker for having created "the tremendous surge of affluence in the last seventy-five years which has lifted the working masses in the developed countries well above any level recorded, even for the well-to-do." [11]

Winslow Taylor's scientific management consisted of replacing rule-of-thumb methods with a scientific method—applying scientific efficiency to tasks, the selection of employees, the supervisions of each worker, and division of work.

Reading that now, you're probably thinking, "Duh." Anyone that's read a single book on management, worked in a company, or simply seen how companies work by watching TV shows can tell you it would be a good idea to apply scientific principles to managing people inside of a company. It doesn't make sense to select employees based on family ties or friends of friends. You can attract more, higher quality applicants, and systematically select the person that's the best fit by requesting and sorting through resumes. A company that adopted those principles would be more likely to succeed than one that just hired their friends.

What seems obvious to us now was a tremendous innovation

at the time. It took Winslow Taylor decades to invent and articulate that process to others.

Now thousands of students at a single university in India will learn it all in a single semester getting their University degree.

Countries like China and India have developed incredible expertise around globalizing technology. They don't need to spend decades developing management theories or new products—they just need to read the book, or more often, photocopy it.

IMPROVING COMMUNICATION TECHNOLOGY: FROM $20 PHONE CARDS TO SKYPE

Recalling a trip to Europe less than twenty years ago, a friend of mine remembered squeezing into a phone booth and scratching the code off of a ten dollar phone card to make a thirty-minute call back to the U.S. On a recent trip to Asia, he made the same call over Skype using free wifi in a cafe while he was having lunch.

The shift moving jobs overseas is also being driven by communication technology which makes it easier to find, hire, and manage remote workers.

Imagine if, ten years ago, you wanted to hire an editor for a magazine you were launching on craft beer. You had to put the word out in your personal network, maybe post the ad to some job boards locally. Then you hoped you got a decent referral for someone that was a talented editor, looking for work, and knew a thing or two about craft beer.

Today, platforms like Elance, UpWork (formerly oDesk), People per Hour, and Freelancer.com now make it possible to hire and manage contract workers from around the world. These companies connect contractors looking for work with employers looking for contractors. Just as Amazon.com lets you browse a massive inventory of products you may never have known existed, new hiring platforms let employers browse through a worldwide listing of potential contractors they might never have known existed.

There were plenty of individuals that were talented editors, looking for work, and knew about craft beer ten years ago, yet it was hard to find them. Today, you can search for them and find a specific person that has "editor" and "craft beer" in their profile.

The same improvements in technology that have made hiring easier also made managing and working with remote teams easier. Online video conferencing has become ubiquitous. Skype pioneered free video calls after launching in 2003 and other software like Google Hangouts and GoToMeeting have followed, making it possible to see and talk with anyone with an internet connection and a smartphone. Which, as of 2015, was 1.75 billion people and rising fast.

Other companies have exploded around remote communication and management. Slack, founded in 2013, was valued at $1 billion within 18 months of their launch. The technology is simple, functioning much like a team chat room. The reason for the company's growth says as much about the demand and use of these sorts of platforms as it does about the company itself.

THE RISE OF THE MICRO-MULTINATIONAL

If you think this doesn't apply to your company or your industry, it's worth looking at just what types of employers now have access to this technology.

Opportunities available only to larger, 500+ person companies just a decade ago in 2005 are as of this writing available to businesses with less than a dozen full-time employees scattered across continents—the rise of a company structure known as "micro-multinational."

Jesse Lawler, an entrepreneur from Los Angeles, runs a software development company called *Evil Genius Technologies* and *Podcast Pop*, which makes customized apps for podcasters. The company, while based out of Los Angeles, has only two American employees. Jesse lives in Vietnam, where around half of his team is based. The rest of his team lives all over the world, from England, to India, to the Philippines.

Jesse is able to structure his team to get the best of all worlds. He has a customer support and sales representative in the U.S. that manages his clients and a development team in Vietnam where he's able to take advantage of high-end computer programming talent at rates Americans and Europeans can't compete with for cost of living reasons alone.

The investments created around fifteen years ago by large Japanese software companies investing in Vietnamese universities paved the way for guys like Jesse to come in and benefit from a well-trained work force at an impressive value.[12]

If his company was based in the U.S., Jesse would be able to employ (at most) one or two developers. It's difficult for small businesses to handle the administrative cost of employing people in the U.S. and the cost in terms of salary is typically at least three to four times higher. Employers like Jesse now have access to a global talent pool.

The company I worked with for two years had a similar structure—a warehouse in a rural part of California where real estate was relatively cheap; sales and customer support in downtown San Diego; a web marketing team in the Philippines and Vietnam; and a manufacturing team in China.

The structure gave us strong, sustainable, competitive advantages over other companies in our industry. Using contractors and employees in Asia, we were able to develop the most effective online marketing in the industry for much less than competitors. Cost advantages of manufacturing in China let us have our cake and eat it too—we could release best-in-class products in terms of quality, yet price them more aggressively than inferior products from competitors.

At a time when many companies were struggling, we were growing at high, double digit rates thanks to these advantages.

An increasingly well trained and more easily accessible workforce in Southeast Asia, South America, and Eastern Europe are eager to do work at wages that provide a high quality of life in their home countries, but are often well below entry level salaries in the West.

Communication and cultural differences still exist and it will take time for those to diffuse globally, but it will happen faster than you expect. Many companies just haven't figured this out. While micro-multinationals are already possible, it will take a little while for businesses to catch up. But given the enormous advantages in productivity it offers, it will.

A word of caution: You may feel that some of these practices are exploitative and unjust; I certainly did, and in some cases, they certainly are.

Yet I would advise you to consider that justice and fairness—seemingly noble concepts in a world where everything is carefully controlled (like your high school, college, or well manicured corporate pamphlet)—are very nebulous concepts in reality.

Regardless of how you feel about the fairness of these practices, they are very real and the effects they have on your life will be just as real. If your job is unfairly and unjustly moved overseas, it's still gone. It's more effective to accept this reality and work to improve it than to bemoan it from the sidelines.

The best way to improve conditions is for individuals with a strong moral compass to acquire power and build better systems. Are democracies more just and fair than dictatorships because the democratic politicians themselves are more just and fair? A quick glance at CNN would seem to discredit that notion. Instead, democracies better distribute the power.[13] An evil, power-hungry president can be impeached. An evil dictator, not so much. The good news, that we'll dig into later, is that today power is more accessible and better distributed than ever.

Every farsighted, high-quality employer (potentially you) that comes in and hires someone at above market rates and invests in them as a valuable part of a team is creating a job for someone that otherwise would have had to work for a low-quality employer. They are also more likely to win out in the long term. While the companies who pay the minimum possible wage and nickel and dime their employees may make a quick buck, they rarely seem to last.

IN SUMMARY (A.K.A. TL;DR)

Improved education standards are taking the implementation of existing best practices and globalizing them.

Improved communication technology has made it easy for individuals and companies to find, hire, and manage not just industrial workers, but knowledge workers.

The number of individuals looking for jobs, hoping to follow someone else's orders, are growing exponentially.

Could your job theoretically be done over an internet connection and phone line?

Yet, your job being outsourced isn't the only threat at hand. Even as globalization moves knowledge jobs overseas, there's increasing pressure at home.

Your Middle Class existence isn't just being squeezed by overseas workers, it's being squeezed by technology being developed just down the street.

CHAPTER 2

THE ACCELERATION OF TECHNOLOGY

All That Is Old Is New Again

VENTURE CAPITALIST FIRMS ARE FAMOUS FOR THEIR investment theses, the basic premise that fuels their investing strategy. These are simple statements which result in the investment of billions of dollars.

Andreessen-Horowitz, a Venture capital firm started by Marc Andreessen and Ben Horowitz, that manages $4 billion as of March 2014, operates on an investment thesis of five words:

Software Is Eating the World.

What is so profound in those five words that it directs how they invest billions of dollars?

The trend Andreessen-Horowitz is betting on may seem new

and disruptive, but it's just the next step in a well-understood process that's been happening for hundreds of years: technological innovation.

Certainly more major businesses and industries—from movies to agriculture to national defense—are being run by software delivered over the internet. Ten years ago, if you wanted to send money to a friend, you had to put the money in an envelope and wrap it in tin foil so they hopefully wouldn't scan it and steal it at the post office or you had to go to Western Union and send it through their office all the while paying exorbitant fees.

Paypal has gotten rid of both of those scenarios with the click of a button.

While the notion that technology is playing an increasingly important role in our lives is not new or surprising, what is new is the scale and scope at which that is true and how fast it's changing.

In 1980, AT&T hired McKinsey & Co—one of the most prestigious management consulting firms in the world—to predict how many cell phone users there would be in the U.S. in 2000. Based on the large study they conducted, they predicted there would be around 900,000.

There were actually about 100 million. So close! Only off by ninety nine million one hundred thousand—a factor of 120.[14]

Because of the internet, and increasingly because of mobile

phones, all of the technology required to transform industries is now available at a global scale. Over two billion people used broadband internet in 2014, up from around 50 million a decade earlier in 2004. Predictions indicate over the course of the next decade as many as five billion people worldwide will own smartphones, giving almost every human on Earth access to the internet all day, every day. If previous track records of such a prediction are an indicator, it may be a lot more, a lot sooner.

While it's not politically correct to talk about, an article in *The New York Times* tells it like it is:

> *An ad in 1967 for an automated accounting system urged companies to replace humans with automated systems that 'can't quit, forget or get pregnant.' Featuring a visibly pregnant, smiling woman leaving the office with baby shower gifts, the ads, which were published in leading business magazines, warned of employees who 'know too much for your own good'—'your good' meaning that of the employer. Why be dependent on humans? 'When Alice leaves, will she take your billing system with her?' the ad pointedly asked, emphasizing that this couldn't be fixed by simply replacing "Alice" with another person.*[15]

This trend has been chronically underestimated. In 2001, Borders agreed to hand over its online business to Amazon because it believed online book sales were "non-strategic and unimportant."

Oops.

Today, Amazon is a software company as well as the world's largest bookseller. As Borders waded through its death throes, Amazon promoted its Kindle digital books over its physical books for the first time. The books themselves are now the machines, a combination of data, hardware, and software.

We can trace this same trend through almost every industry.

When was the last time you went to rent a movie from an employee at a movie rental store? Not since Netflix blind-sided Blockbuster.

How about buying an album from an employee at a record store? Probably not since iTunes, Spotify and Pandora—all software companies—ate up 29% of total revenue in the industry in 2010, up from 2% in 2004.

Had any photos developed lately by someone with a job at Kodak? Probably not since Kodak went out of business and was replaced by Shutterfly, Snapfish, and Flickr.

LinkedIn is also eating away at jobs traditionally held by recruiters.

Even jobs in companies and industries that seem more traditional are disappearing. Wal-Mart and FedEx are primarily networked logistics companies powered by software and internal processes.[16] While it may need people to handle many of those processes today, how much longer will that be the case?

MOORE'S LAW: ON THE DANGER'S OF LINEAR THINKING IN AN EXPONENTIAL WORLD

In a nonchalant article published in 1965, Intel co-founder Gordon Moore described a trend he'd observed happening within Intel. Computer power was doubling every eighteen to twenty-four months.

The formulation, now called Moore's Law,[17] has held true for the last half century. If computing power continues to double and costs continue to halve every 18 to 24 months, we're in the middle of an exponential graph.

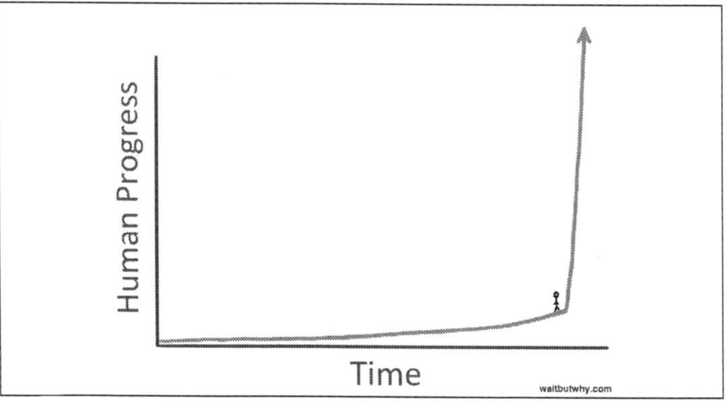

http://waitbutwhy.com/2015/01/artificial-intelligence-revolution-1.html

When the Human Genome Project began in 1990, it took seven years of costly labor and employing the smartest scientists in the field to sequence the first 1% of the human genome. Many critics fought to cancel the project, arguing it would take too long and was too expensive. But instead of taking another seven years to sequence the next 1%, it took a single year. In the next year they doubled again, from 2% to 4%. The trend continued and the project was completed in fifteen years. A project that took seven years to reach one percent completion, was finished in 15 years total. 99% of the project was done in about half that time.

It's worth remembering that the folks at McKinsey & Co and the people who wanted to cancel the human genome project were some of the most intelligent, best educated people on Earth. Yet, they didn't understand the implications of exponential growth.

Not because they weren't smart, but because humans evolved to live in a linear, biological world, a world dramatically different from the one we live in now.

To get an idea of the impact this could have on jobs and our economy, look at the effect of the Industrial Revolution, which created a 1–2% compounding growth rate of income for around two hundred years.

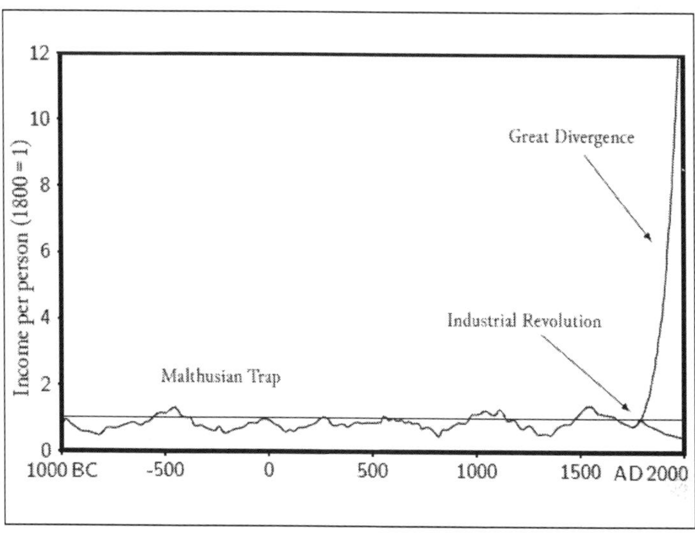

http://themisescircle.org/features/files/2013/04/world-economic-history.png

Since the inception of Moore's Law, that rate of improvement for computers has reached 40%—twenty to forty times, or 2,000% to 4,000%, of what we saw after the Industrial Revolution.

The notion of software eating the world is the latest in a long line of technological innovations we've seen since the start of the Industrial Revolution. The story of the Industrial Revolution in the 18th and 19th centuries and the Knowledge Revolution in the 20th is the proliferation of technology and the growth that accompanied it.

Both the growth in technology and globalization are continuing at an accelerating rate. Many people are responding by further investing in credentials. Let's see how that's working out.

CHAPTER 3

THE COMMODITIZATION OF CREDENTIALISM

Why MBAs and JDs Can't Get Jobs

> *"It's never been worse to be information smart than it is today."*
>
> – GARY VAYNERCHUK AT SXSW, 2014

Angie graduated from law school in 2013. It wasn't a so-called top tier law school, but it was well-respected. I was sitting with her in a hamburger joint while she related to me that she spent a year waiting tables before she got enough connections to finally "get lucky" and land a job at a law firm.

I'm betting you know someone like Angie.

Even as the rate of unemployment has improved gradually

following the 2008 financial collapse, what's frequently ignored are the people who are underemployed, settling for part-time jobs or who have given up looking altogether.

According to the Bureau of Labor Statistics, six years after that Recession ended, the unemployment rate was still in the double digits: 11.2%.[18]

Why, six years after a recession, are so many people unable to find jobs?

We've already addressed two reasons: many of the jobs are going overseas or being replaced by machines.

Yet shouldn't there be more jobs for the better educated? The number of college graduates has been steadily climbing since the 1940s and is at an all-time high. Why aren't they landing jobs with their degrees?

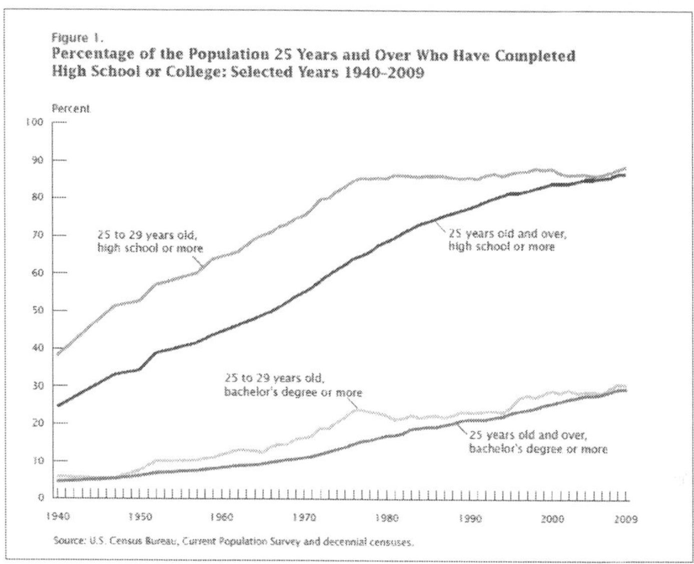

http://www.ajeforum.com/wp-content/uploads/2012/11/121129-Sensenig-fig-2.jpg

A paper published by the New York Federal Reserve stated: "[I]ndividuals just beginning their careers often need time to transition into the labor market. Still, the percentage who are unemployed or 'underemployed' has risen, particularly since the 2001 recession." [19]

These are people like Landon and Megan, employees at the Atlanta-based law firm which requires everyone on staff, even the file clerk, to have a college degree because "it's a buyer's market for employers." [20]

Have we passed the point where a basic college degree is enough? Perhaps what you need is a graduate degree?

In 2014 the overall employment rate for recent law school grads fell for the sixth year in a row to 84.5 percent according to a report from the National Association for Law Placement. While the overall number of jobs increased, law school class graduation sizes are growing faster than the demand for the lawyers.[21]

As Landon's and Megan's stories illustrate, even for individuals with an advanced degree who are able to get a job, the value of a degree is dropping.

In a 2012 study done by PayScale, which collects salary data from individuals with MBAs through online pay-comparison tools, results showed that median salaries had stalled over the past four years. More significantly, the value of the MBA over the course of a career has stalled.[22]

While everyone can relate and recognize that there's a shortage of jobs for highly-credentialed individuals, no one seems to have a clear answer for why that is. The glut of lawyers in the U.S. may be the most obvious example, but even in the traditional STEM fields (science, technology, engineering, and mathematics), which were long considered lock-ins for employment, people with related degrees are struggling harder to find jobs than they were a decade ago.

Jobs in almost all industries are becoming increasingly commoditized. It makes sense to us that low-skilled jobs with lower barriers to entry are being affected by globalization and technology, but why is it affecting the more highly-credentialed ones?

THE CYNEFIN FRAMEWORK AND YOUR CAREER

The Cynefin framework[23] (pronounced Kih-*neh*-vihn) was developed by Dave Snowden after studying the management structure at IBM. The framework became popular, and was featured in publications including the Harvard Business Review.[24] It divides work and management up in ways that are more effective given the changing nature of work.

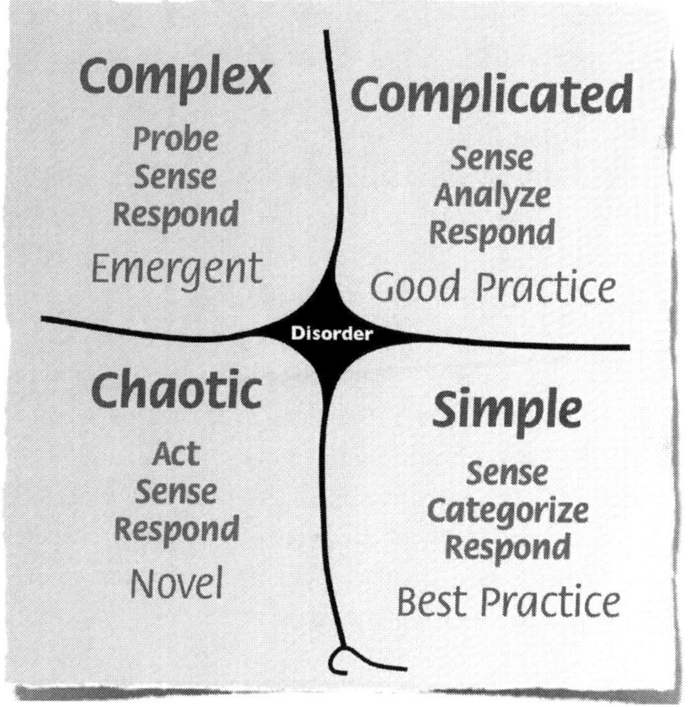

https://upload.wikimedia.org/wikipedia/commons/4/45/Cynefin_framework_Feb_2011.jpeg

It categorizes work and management into four separate domains: simple, complicated, complex, and chaotic. When we traditionally look at a job, we might say that someone needs a high school degree or a college degree or a graduate degree. This categorization of work is effective along a straight line from simple to complicated. A complicated problem would require further education to solve, while a simple problem would require relatively less.

What this categorization ignores, however, are the complex and chaotic domains. Historically this may have been acceptable—pretty much all work has fallen on the simple to complicated line. But in recent years that's no longer the case.

The *Simple* domain is the one where the relationship between cause and effect is obvious; anyone can apply a best practice to solve a simple problem. It's something that can be easily documented, like the instructions for putting together an Ikea table or a set of Legos.

The *Complicated* domain is where the relationship between cause and effect requires analysis and investigation. Operating in a complicated domain requires investigation and/or the application of expert knowledge. It's something that requires thinking and consideration, but getting it done can be handled by utilizing existing expertise. This is the domain you are equipped to deal with coming out of school.

Complex is where the relationships between cause and effect are only clear in retrospect. It's an emergent practice. This is the field that entrepreneurs frequently find themselves in. It's not clear what to do next, because you exhausted the expertise you gained through education. The problem is solved, instead, by testing new solutions and seeing the reaction.

Chaotic is the domain where there is no relationship between cause and effect. We must act in spite of the disorder, to develop ways to survive. In his book, *The Hard Thing About Hard Things*, venture capitalist and former CEO Ben Horowitz recounts taking his company public during the 2001 crash. In the midst of layoffs and and sales falling off a cliff as the tech bubble crashed, he had to convince investors they should put more money into the company. There's no guide book for that nor college course.

Over the course of the 20th century, we've started moving the workforce around the Cynefin graph. The rise of credentialism was the result of a need to train people to operate in the complicated domain. In a world where the solution can be found by using existing expertise, it made a lot of sense to develop a system for evaluating people based on their levels of education.

As discussed before, the simple and complicated can be reduced to step-by-step instructions like putting together Legos. This makes them teachable, and the modern education system evolved to be very effective at that.

Horace Mann, often credited as the father of the modern education system, started a school one-hundred-and-fifty years ago, called the Common School. The purpose of the common school was to teach students how to follow directions effectively so they would be prepared for factory work.

A few years after the school opened, Mann realized that he had a shortage of teachers for the Common School, so he started the Normal School. The Normal School was where teachers were trained before going to give classes at the Common School. We needed *normal* teachers to train students to be *common.*

The modern educational system is built on the back of this premise—creating *normal, common* workers. In 1900, factory workers were in demand and being trained to be common or normal was valuable. We needed to train kids to do what they were told and sit still and listen to instructions and say them back to us.

Times have changed. It's now less valuable than ever to understand how to follow directions and implement best practices.

It's the work of understanding and operating in the complex and chaotic systems—*entrepreneurship*—that's increasingly in demand.

Individuals looking to implement best practices can't create growth in most businesses, so they aren't in demand. In the situations where they can, they are being quickly replaced by and competing with machines and a globalized work force.

SECTION

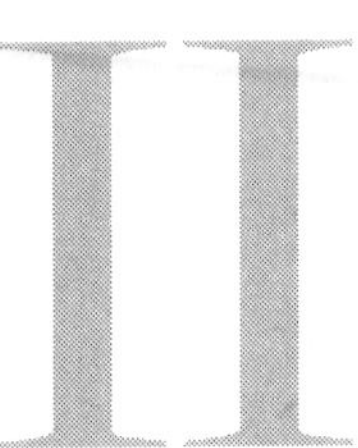

Why Are We at the End of Jobs?

(Or How Limits Work)

In the 1980s, Creative Output, an Israeli company, developed the first software package that sped up scheduling for production environments like a typical factory floor.

In the process of setting up and installing the software, one of Creative Output's founders, Eli Goldratt, found that frequently the software failed to live up to its potential because of the existing habits of employees and managers.

Despite the software offering them obvious solutions to speeding up the factory and increasing output, the pre-existing paradigms and mental models of the managers kept them from implementing the software successfully.

Goldratt, frustrated by the inefficiency, holed up for 13 months to write *The Goal*, which laid out his "Theory of Constraints." Goldratt's theory explains that any system with a goal has one limit, and worrying about anything other than that limit is a waste of resources.

If an assembly has three sections, and two of those sections can produce one hundred units per hour while the third can only produce fifty units per hour, any investment outside of improving the third section won't improve the outcome. Doubling the first two to make two hundred units per hour while the third still only produces fifty units per hour will only yield fifty units per hour.

If you've ever helped send out a physical mail campaign, there's always a clear bottleneck. If you have five people stuffing envelopes at a rate of one hundred envelopes per hour (twenty envelopes per hour for each person) and one person addressing them at a rate of fifty units per hour, the envelopes will pile up and you'll be waiting around on the one person to address all the envelopes.

Adding five more people to stuff envelopes won't get the job done any faster, the envelopes will just pile up faster.

Adding a single person to address the envelopes will get the job done in half the time since it addresses the bottleneck. 100 envelopes will get stuffed every hour and 100 envelopes will get addressed.

This is obvious in simple systems like stuffing envelopes, but equally true and far more powerful in complicated and complex systems.

If you're trying to grow a business, there's always a primary limit preventing that. If you have an amazing product and no one knows about it, improving the product won't help it sell more.

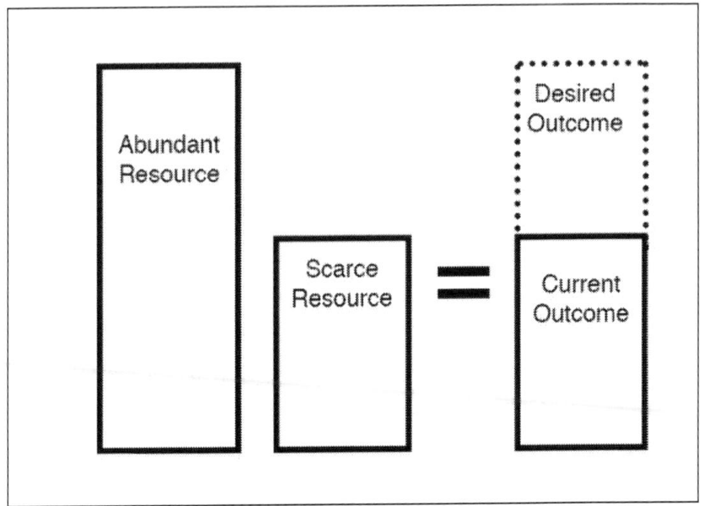

Source: The Fourth Economy – Ron Davison

Limits play an enormous role in any system, from our day-to-day lives to how economies work.

There are three basic questions to ask when applying Goldratt's framework:

1. What's the system?
2. What's the current limit?
3. What's the obvious way to improve the limit?

Once you can identify the components of a system and discover what the limit is, figuring out how to improve it becomes much easier.

While our first instinct is usually attempting to push harder, it's more valuable to figure out *where* to push.

The famous dictum, "If I had an hour to solve a problem, I would spend 59 minutes asking the right questions," recognizes that defining the system and its limit often makes the solution obvious.

THE SECRET TO HEALTH: MORE SLEEP, FEWER SCONES

Let's apply the framework to something almost everyone's experienced. You've made it your New Year's resolution to get in shape. This is the year that you're finally going to get healthy. We've got our outcome: Get healthy.

So you join the gym, put together a workout plan, and order all the right supplements. You've got protein powder, creatine, and everything else you read about on the internet that you need to get in shape.

You stick to the workout plan. You hit the gym six days a week. After a couple of days, you haven't noticed any improvements. You keep going. After a month, still nothing.

Before we go and do a lot more hard work to improve our health (the system we defined), let's take Goldratt's and Edison's advice and answer the next two questions.

What's the limit?

What's the obvious way to improve it?

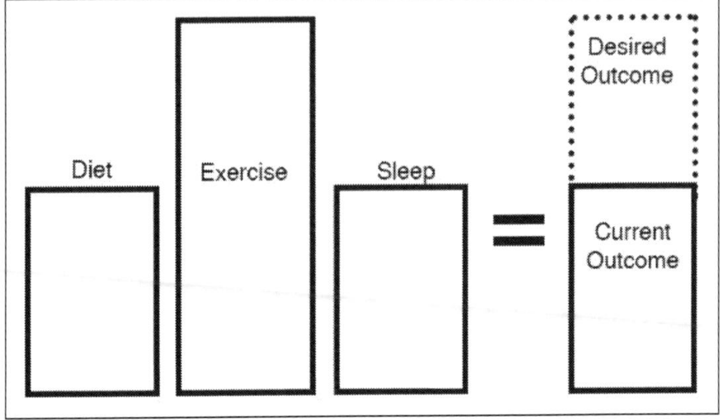

While you're going to the gym six days a week, you're going at 5am, which means most days you only sleep five or six hours if you were up late the night before. You also treat yourself to a scone from Starbucks after every workout.

An hour running on the treadmill will burn 400 calories. A scone from Starbucks has 400 calories, which means you're not going to lose any weight. Any hormonal benefits of exercise are being counteracted by the hormonal problems caused by a lack of sleep. You're spending more and more time exercising when the limit isn't exercise.

If you fix your sleep and diet, then you'll get better results even with less exercise. By giving up the scone and getting an extra couple hours of sleep every night, even with a very modest amount of exercise, you start to see the pounds drop off. Instead of spending two hours in the gym every day, an hour in the gym every other day suddenly yields better results because you've addressed the appropriate limits.

Despite playing year-round sports in high school and college football for two years, I was grossly overweight, weighing 345 pounds at my heaviest. Some days I would have to get in bed for an hour in the afternoon just to relieve the back pain from carrying around so much excess fat.

I was working out five or six days a week and taking around 30–50 pills of supplements a day. In order to manage playing sports, studying, and working a part-time job as a tutor, I was throwing out everything else in my life. I never cooked for myself, preferring a steady diet of foot-longs from Subway and family packs from KFC and sleeping around five or six hours a night.

Watching my mother go through a double hip replacement convinced me something was going to give sooner or later. I was on a one-way train to dysfunctional living at twenty-two years old. I cut my workout schedule in half, often exercising only a day or two per week, started sleeping seven to eight hours a night, and eating a diet of lean meat and vegetables that I cooked at home. I still remember stepping on the scale and seeing 220 pounds, 125 pounds down from my heaviest, and thinking the scale must have been broken.

Limits can be applied to any system in order to dramatically improve the outcome without having to dramatically improve the inputs. I didn't add more time in my life to be healthy, I just changed the limits that I was addressing with the time I already had available.

"Give me a lever long enough...and I shall move the world." Addressing the limit is like having a longer lever. Instead of just pushing harder, we're figuring out where to push to create the greatest impact.

HOW LIMITS WORK IN ECONOMIES AND CAREERS

Over the past seven hundred years, the West has seen an unprecedented level of growth. Sitting on the dirt floor of their hut in 1300, a European peasant couldn't imagine the quality of life most middle class Americans enjoy today.

Our rapid improvements have only been possible because at three distinct points in our recent history, we have, as a society, figured out the limit to economic progress and shifted to re-address it.

The most recent was when the limit shifted to require more complicated work. The Baby Boomer generation went to school and got the expertise and credentials to address that limit. It's for that reason we enjoy the level of affluence we have today.

The limit has moved again from complicated work (jobs) to complex and chaotic work (entrepreneurship). Despite being more credentialed than ever, the U.S. economy has gone from adding 2.5 million jobs per year between 1960 and 2000, to shedding jobs at a rate of 100,000 in the first decade of the 21st century. Growth hasn't just slowed—it's reversed.

In his book, *The Fourth Economy*, author and systems thinker Ron Davison organizes the last seven hundred years of Western History into three distinct economic periods: Agricultural (1300–1700), Industrial (1700–1900), and Knowledge (1900–2000).[25]

At each economic transition, we've seen diminishing returns from investing in the previous limit. The popular response has been to label our current economic woes a painful global recession. The popular point of view is wrong. We aren't going through a global recession—we're transitioning between two distinct economic periods.

Certainly, the model of four distinct periods is certainly oversimplified. Economies and societies are far more complex systems than an assembly line. Different limits can exist in the same society. There are still agricultural workers (farmers) and industrial workers throughout the West, but the broadest segment of Western population is employed in the knowledge economy, and it's that part of the economy that, over the past hundred years, has been responsible for creating most of the abundance and wealth now available.

When the limit of an economy shifts through the four different stages, investing more heavily in what has always worked won't improve the output—just as spending more time in the gym is counter-productive if you aren't sleeping enough or eating healthy. If you push harder and harder on a shorter and shorter lever, you still won't get better results.

In order to understand how limits work in economics and how it affects your career choice, let's take a (brief) look at what has happened over the past seven hundred years of Western History and how we arrived where we are today.

THE AGRICULTURAL ECONOMY (1300–1700): HENRY'S HERESY

Starting in around the year 1300, natural resources were the primary source of wealth in the West. The wealthiest people were those that had the most natural resources because they owned the land. Land was the limit.

The nations that thrived in Medieval Europe did precisely that. Beginning with the Portuguese in the early 1400s and then eventually all major Western European powers, the Age of Discovery was characterized by the rapid and dramatic accumulation of land. As these countries and the individuals within them acquired more and more land, they became more powerful and wealthy.

The Catholic Church, which had been the dominant institution in Europe, and the Pope, who had been the dominant player, were eclipsed by a slightly larger group: the rulers of nation-states. Kings. Power transferred from the Church to the Nation-State, and from the Pope to Kings.

Perhaps no individual did more to create the Agricultural Economy than Henry VIII of England. He removed tariffs, made England a free trade zone, and standardized weights and measures to facilitate trade. On continental Europe, merchants moving across Germany would have been faced with hundreds of tariffs, various measurement standards, and different currencies. The same merchant moving across England would have a set of standard weights and measures, and be comparatively tariff free.

He furthered England's policy of emphasizing property rights, which encouraged farmers to invest in their land. This increased the productivity, nutrition, size, and health of individuals. It also created an incentive for them to defend their own land—free men fight harder than serfs.

In the Dark Ages, Kings were subject to the Pope, and in order for Henry to get a divorce he needed papal approval. When Henry's first wife, Catherine, was unable to produce a male heir, Henry wanted a new wife who could.

He petitioned the Pope for a divorce, but when Henry's then-mistress, Anne Boleyn, became pregnant, his hand was forced and he divorced Catherine. Pope Clement excommunicated him. Instead of crawling back to Clement, Henry instead declared himself the head of the Church of England.

Now the head of the Church, Henry proceeded to dissolve Catholic Monasteries and distribute their land through sales and titles to the gentry class. This made the land more productive and generated more money for England, a nation state, instead of the Catholic Church.

The Treaty of Westphalia, signed over one hundred years later in 1648, delivered the *coup de grace*, giving nation states sovereignty over the Church by letting monarchs dictate religion to their subjects. Land had been overcome as a limit, nation-states had eclipsed the Church, and kings had eclipsed the Pope.

From 1300 until around 1700, we went through the first primary economic transition in the West. It consisted of three important characteristics that all future transitions would have:

1. The limit shifted—The Pope's religious authority was not as powerful as the newly established limit: land. With the revenue from the land and the power he was able to distribute to the gentry class, Henry didn't need papal approval to rule.

2. The dominant institution shifted—Because nation states controlled land, the power shifted from the Church to Nation States.

3. The dominant player shifted—Because kings ruled nation states, power shifted from a single individual, the Pope, to a small group, Kings.

Economy	First	Second	Third	Fourth
Period	1300 – 1700	1700 – 1900	1900 – 2000	2000 ~
Limit to Progress	Land	Capital	Knowledge Workers	Entrepreneurship
Type of Economy	Agricultural	Industrial	Information	Entrepreneurial
Intellectual Revolution	Renaissance	Enlightenment	Pragmatism	Systems Thinking
Big Social Invention	Nation-state	Bank	Corporation	Self
Social Revolution	Religion	Politics	Finance	Business

Through King Henry's experiences we start to see the long-lasting impact of being among the first to address a change in limits. England's ascension to the top of the hierarchy among nation states would last until World War I wrought enough destruction in Western Europe that the United States and then the USSR surpassed it.

THE INDUSTRIAL ECONOMY (1700–1900): THE RISE OF THE ROTHSCHILDS

In the three and a half centuries following Henry's rule, the world was transformed. The West went from an agricultural to an industrial economy.

The limit shifted from land to capital, the dominant institution shifted from Nation-States to Banks, and the dominant player shifted from Kings to bankers.

This transformation is best told through the story of Nathan Rothschild, a banker, and Friedrich Wilhelm III, the King of Prussia.

In Medieval Europe, Catholic law prohibited usury, the lending of money at interest. This meant a lot of Jews ended up becoming bankers, as Catholics were effectively forbidden from the job.

The most successful banker was a Jew by the name of Mayer Rothschild. Rothschild saw that there was an opportunity to distribute his five sons across Europe to create an international banking organization at a time when only Jews were bankers and there was relatively little competition.

Nathan Rothschild, the son he sent to London, achieved the most success. Nathan capitalized on the Napoleonic Wars at the turn of the 19th century by buying bonds from the British government—who needed money to fight the war—and then selling those bonds into the international market through his brothers in Vienna, Paris, Frankfurt, and Naples. Brokering the sale of these bonds made the Rothschilds fantastically rich. Richer, in fact, than kings.

As the Napoleonic Wars drew to a close, the Prussian King Friedrich Wilhelm III turned to the Rothschilds for a loan. Napoleon had set off an arms race after his escape from prison and return to France. Prussia needed to modernize and re-arm to defend against Napoleon. The rearmament, which would bring about the formation of modern-day Germany, required a king (Friedrich) to ask a banker (Nathan Rothschild) for a loan.

Despite owning an enormous amount of land, Friedrich lacked the capital to re-arm Prussia.

When Nathan Rothschild received Friedrich's request for a loan, he sent Wilhelm a letter with a *conditional* "Yes." The Rothschilds would loan Germany the money, but only if Friedrich, the king, submitted to a parliamentary form of government in which power was more evenly distributed and corruption more difficult. Nathan wanted to make sure he got his money back, and Parliaments have a lot harder time building palaces for themselves than kings.

A banker dictated terms to a king. What Napoleon failed to do with an army of hundreds of thousands, a banker did with a letter.

The bank was eclipsing the nation-state. Bankers were becoming more powerful than monarchs.

Just like in previous transitions, three fundamental changes had occurred.

1. The limit shifted—Friedrich had land in abundance, but didn't have capital. The limit was capital.

2. The dominant institution shifted—Because banks control capital, the power shifted from nation-states to

banks. Banks controlled the scarce resource and so they gained power.

3. The dominant player shifted—Banks are run by bankers and so bankers became the fundamentally powerful group.

The Rothschilds again show the value of investing early and heavily in a change in limits. No one has heard much about the Rothschilds' banking innovations in the last hundred years or so, yet there are plenty of wealthy Rothschild descendants walking around today.

THE KNOWLEDGE ECONOMY (1900–2000): THE CONQUEST OF THE CORPORATION

Over the course of the one hundred and fifty years following the Napoleonic Wars and Nathan Rothschild's loan to Friedrich, (roughly 1800–1950), the modern corporation arose.

As we transitioned from an industrial to knowledge economy, banks became extremely effective at producing capital, but the economy didn't have enough knowledge to grow. The limit has moved from capital to knowledge. The dominant player changed from banker to CEO, and the dominant institution shifted from banks to corporations.

The story of the shift from an Industrial Economy is best told through the history of J.P. Morgan's bank, Morgan Stanley, and Thomas Watson's corporation, IBM.

Morgan's bank, Morgan Stanley, was the primary bank of Watson's corporation, IBM, in the 1970's.

Just as Morgan Stanley was one of the great symbols and controllers of capital, IBM was one of the great symbols and controllers of knowledge. From the suit and tie dress code (showing that their workers were unfit for manual work), to the company's slogan of "THINK," IBM was symbolically the home of knowledge.

For most of the 20th century, corporations like IBM did not antagonize their banks. They were faithful and monogamous. Because financial markets were opaque and difficult to understand for corporations, it was difficult to get all the information needed to operate effectively in them.

Banks still held the power. Corporations needed bankers who controlled the information about how financial markets worked to advise them.

When IBM issued a billion dollars in bonds in 1975, it told Morgan Stanley that it wanted to bring in Salomon Brothers to help with the issue—a move that was, at the time, unprecedented. Bond issues were typically always handled by a single bank. Not wanting to lose their hegemonic position as IBM's sole bank, Morgan Stanley refused to cooperate with Salomon. IBM, intimidated but not deterred, went ahead without Morgan Stanley.

The bond issue was a success and a new precedent was set. The scales tipped. Banking went from a relationship-based business to a transactional one. It became commoditized and, in time, the corporation transcended the bank as the dominant institution. Corporations now began to dictate terms to banks. CEOs began to dictate terms to bankers. The demand for knowledge eclipsed the demand for capital. Banks were subjugated to corporations in a way that they never had been before.

Again, we see the value of investing early. Despite what many would say have been substantial blunders over the past thirty years (including handing Microsoft over to Bill Gates), IBM is still a tremendously valuable company, with a market capitalization of around $170 billion as of 2015.

We see again the three changes in all preceding transitions:

1. The limit shifted—Morgan Stanley had capital in abundance, but didn't have knowledge. The limit was knowledge.

2. The dominant institution shifted—Because corporations controlled knowledge, the power shifted from banks to corporations.

3. The dominant player shifted—Corporations are run by CEOs, and so CEOs became the fundamentally powerful class.

THE ASCENDENCE OF THE ENTREPRENEUR

In every previous transition, three shifts have taken place.

In the current transition (the Fourth Economy), that looks like this:

1. The limit is shifting from knowledge to entrepreneurship. The entrepreneurial Complex and Chaotic domains are the ones increasingly in demand.

2. The dominant institution is shifting from Corporation to the Individual (or self). What used to require large companies, technology, and globalization has now been made available to the individual or micro-multinational.

3. The dominant player is shifting from CEO to Entrepreneur.

Most institutions and individuals don't have a good track record of adapting effectively to these shifts. They continue working to address the wrong limit decades or even centuries later. We're seeing that now.

Individuals are investing in more knowledge, they're going back to school to get more credentials. Even as the returns on credentials are declining, still students continue to pay more and more for them. Considering credentials and knowledge have been the scarce resource for the last century, this isn't surprising. For the past one hundred years, going back to school for more credentials was a good strategy.

Yet, even as the cost of college and graduate school increases each year, the value is decreasing.

Simple supply and demand shows us that investing more

in abundant resources isn't a very good strategy. It won't improve the outcome of a system. Spending more time in the gym won't make you any healthier if you aren't sleeping or eating well.

However, it takes society a long time to adapt to the shift and make wise investments. What seems obvious in retrospect appears, at the time, a risky investment.

While it takes society as a whole a long time to shift and address the limit, there is always a golden moment when it's easier, safer, and more profitable than widely perceived to invest in a scarce resource.

Henry invested in land and England, a small island in the North Sea became the dominant world power for a few hundred years. The Rothschilds invested in capital when most people undervalued it, and to this day are among the richest families in Europe. Thomas Watson invested in knowledge by founding IBM when it was undervalued and built one of the defining corporations of the twentieth century.

Could we be at the same point for entrepreneurship?

CHAPTER 4

THE ENTREPRENEURIAL ECONOMY (2000ISH–???)

The Emergence of the Entrepreneur

GLOBALIZATION MEANS YOU ARE NO LONGER COMPETING to be more knowledgeable than the person down the street, but more knowledgeable than seven billion people around the world. Communication technology and increasing education standards have brought more individuals into the knowledge economy in the past ten years than in the preceding century. We've seen the number of college graduates globally go from ninety million to one hundred and thirty million between 2000 and 2010. It took us all of human history to get to ninety million and then only ten years to add another forty million.[26]

Secondly, the rapid advance of technology has replaced many

simple tasks and driven more people into complicated knowledge work.

More than half of America's recent college graduates are either unemployed or working in a job that doesn't require a bachelor's degree. In 2014, the overall employment rate for law school graduates fell for the sixth consecutive year. It would appear that knowledge is no longer the scarce resource it was one hundred years ago.

Yet credentialism, a system for measuring knowledge, has continued to grow dramatically. The number of college graduates has been climbing steadily since the 1940s and shows no signs of slowing down.

Here's a thought experiment. Look at your local community and ask yourself: which of the following would create more growth?

Ten times more capital? Never has capital been more readily available than it is today.

What about ten times more knowledge in the form of college graduates or lawyers or doctors or MBAs? Would that create growth? We're in the middle of that experiment now and it doesn't appear to be paying off.

What about ten times more entrepreneurship?

HOW TO MAKE DECISIONS LIKE A BILLIONAIRE

> *"A few major opportunities, clearly recognizable as such, will usually come to one who continuously searches and waits, with a curious mind loving diagnosis involving multiple variables. And then all that is required is a willingness to bet heavily when the odds are extremely favorable, using resources available as a result of prudence and patience in the past."*
>
> – CHARLES T. MUNGER

Frequently overshadowed by Warren Buffett, his partner in the $300 billion Berkshire Hathaway holding company, Charlie Munger is a quiet, reclusive figure. Rarely making public appearances, the unostentatious billionaire spends most of his time as Buffett does: reading, thinking, and managing Berkshire Hathaway from his home in Southern California.

Buffett and Munger have, over the course of their careers, amassed a multi-billion dollar empire with a brilliant-in-its-simplicity investment strategy: value investing.

Value investing—as practiced by the duo of billionaires—is a process of evaluating the underlying value of a company as if they owned it, adding in a margin of error, and then looking at what the current market price of it is.

If they value a company for an intrinsic value of a billion dollars and the stock price reflects a valuation of two hundred million dollars, they're likely to take a heavy position in that company, knowing that over time, the market will eventually correct its valuation. As the pair only invests when planning on holding the stock for a long time, they're apt to reap the eight-hundred-million-dollar market misjudgment whenever the market corrects.

More notable than what value investing is, however, is what it *isn't*.

It rejects many of the basic precepts most investment managers subscribe to.

The pair don't try to beat the market on a yearly basis, instead focusing on forty-year time frames. They don't invest in technology stocks. They certainly don't day trade.

They also don't diversify. In Buffett's words: "Diversification is protection against ignorance. It makes little sense if you know what you are doing." Instead of diversifying, they focus on identifying "a few major opportunities" and betting heavily on them. Munger attributes the majority of their fifty billion dollars to "perhaps four or five investments" over the course of a five-decade career. You don't need more than a handful of ten billion dollar decisions to make a world-class career.

Simplistic in its brilliance, brutal in its simplicity, a test of willpower and patience in its execution, no one has come close to matching Buffett and Munger as value investors.

CAN YOU ACQUIRE ENTREPRENEURSHIP?

We're at a transition point from knowledge to entrepreneurial work. The individuals who will gain the most from the transition are those that invest early and heavily in Entrepreneurship just as the Rothschilds benefitted from investing early and heavily in capital, and IBM benefited from investing early and heavily in knowledge.

So how do you invest in Entrepreneurship?

Beyond being helpful for figuring out the obvious thing to do, limits empower us because they transform events into processes. Thinking in limits is process thinking, not event thinking.

When we define something as an event, as yes or no—healthy or unhealthy, wealthy or poor, happy or unhappy, entrepreneurial or not—we've usually defined it too broadly to make any progress.

While almost no one knows how to be perfectly healthy, everyone knows one thing they can do to get healthier. Instead of being paralyzed by the perceived inability to reach a far-off final destination or goal, the people that succeed in getting healthier are the ones that start taking small steps in the right direction. They start eating a healthy breakfast each morning or going to the gym one day per week. Eventually breakfast turns into lunch and dinner and one day per week turns into three, and over the course of a year, a tremendous amount of progress has been made.

This is just as true of the skills we need in our careers. The task of becoming a doctor wasn't clear one hundred years ago—in fact, it seemed overwhelming:

How do I get into a university? What do I have to do to get into med school?

Now there are standards for all those things. If you're in college then you know you need to take biology and chemistry classes and get a 3.X GPA to be admitted to medical school.

Over the course of the 20th century, we've developed credentialism as a way to define how much knowledge there is. There are a lot of letters we can put after our name and plaques that we can put on our wall to show how much knowledge we have as a resource. Credentialism made it clear what the next step was and how much progress we'd made thus far.

Entrepreneurship is a skillset which can be acquired.

Yet asking, "Am I an entrepreneur?" isn't a helpful question.

We typically don't think of entrepreneurship as a resource. It's relatively easy to figure out how much land or capital someone has, but we don't think entrepreneurship is as easily quantifiable or defined.

Entrepreneurship is a skill set, a resource that can be acquired and invested in, just like acquiring stock in a company or acquiring knowledge credentials. We think of acquiring knowledge or skills—like product management or sales or marketing—as resources, but we still don't think of entrepreneurship that way.

Right now, there's no way to measure entrepreneurship. No one would ever write "two years' experience in entrepreneurship" on their resume. If we imagine a knowledge worker trying to invest in entrepreneurship, there are clear paths to moving from doing knowledge work to doing entrepreneurial work.

Role	Knowledge	Entrepreneurship
Experienced Founder	0%	100%
Early Stage Founder	10%	90%
Consultant	20%	80%
Freelancer	30%	70%
Apprentice	40%	60%
Employee with a Side Hustle	60%	40%
Corporate Executive	70%	30%
Entrepreneurial Employee	80%	20%
Non-Entrepreneurial Employee	100%	0%

The chart is admittedly grossly oversimplified and based on a zero sum system indicating the amount each role operates in knowledge work as opposed entrepreneurship. It's intent is not to necessarily categorize the roles, but to show potential paths into entrepreneurship.

Based on the chart, a non-entrepreneurial employee might be someone working at Starbucks or McDonald's whose role is based on following a predetermined script or rule book.

Meanwhile, an entrepreneurial employee may be someone in a traditional corporate structure attempting to innovate within the company by proposing new initiatives and operating with some degree of autonomy.

This hierarchy is semantic and arbitrary, and these definitions are imperfect. You can have corporate executives that are far more entrepreneurial than founders in how they approach their work.

A corporate executive that starts new divisions or spins off a company from inside an existing company is more entrepreneurial than someone owning an equity stake and merely following the directions of their partners.

Freelancers that take no initiative to build new systems that improve their work or sales process could be less entrepreneurial than an employee with a side hustle that's making it happen.

These are simply generalizations intended to demonstrate that although there's not a name for it, you can invest in entrepreneurship as a skill set just like you can knowledge.

INVESTING IN ENTREPRENEURSHIP

Once we see entrepreneurship as an asset or resource that can be invested in, we can apply similar, basic economic concepts towards it and start making better, more reasoned decisions.

If you're buying a traditional stock, you always know how much you can go buy a share of a certain company for. You can plug it into Google and see, down to the cent, what a share in a given company is valued at.

If we're talking about entrepreneurship or knowledge as resources, however, the buy price isn't so easily quantifiable. You can't go to eTrade and buy a share of entrepreneurship or knowledge. Instead, we invest in them with life decisions. Choosing to get an apprenticeship working in an entrepreneurial company instead of going to work in a major corporation is a major career investment decision. Choosing to take ownership of a complex project instead of saying "that's not my job" is an investment decision.

Going back and investing $150,000 to get a MBA is a decision that will impact not just the two years you spend in the program, but the decade after it.

You will be qualified for certain positions and have access to them because of people you may have met in the program. But there's an opportunity cost: you won't have access to or qualify for other positions.

You'll have debt which you'll have to make payments on. That will make it difficult to take an apprenticeship position that pays less, but will get you experience and contacts in an industry you'd like to work in.

THE MONEY IS MADE ON THE BUY

Business brokers are fond of saying that the money is made on the buy. Markets, while not perfectly accurate, will generally correct over time. You know the value of a 2012 Honda Pilot is $15,000, but you find someone that is moving out of the country and in a hurry to sell it and will take $12,000. You know you can hold onto it and wait until someone who will buy it for $15,000 comes along.

This is what Munger and Buffett did when investing in stocks. It's what the Rothschilds did in capital with banking, and what IBM did in knowledge. They invested early and reaped the rewards as markets corrected.

At the turn of the 20th century, when people like employees of IBM invested in the knowledge economy by getting a degree, it wasn't entirely clear to that generation what the value of knowledge was. In society at large, a college degree didn't command the level of respect it does today.

Andrew Youderian now runs not only an eCommerce store selling CB Radios, but also a site named eCommerce Fuel, which is a community for other ecommerce store owners. He spent the first few years of his career working as an investment banker.

He chose to quit his job to run an eCommerce store, not because he thought it would be more profitable, but for the same reason many people in his position do: he wanted to build a lifestyle that would let him spend more time travelling and be with his family.

Though he didn't expect it at the time he quit, he had lunch with a former colleague years later and discovered that, in his best year of running his own business, he had made more than his investment banker friend.

As his former colleagues continued putting in 50–80 hours per week for fifty weeks a year, Andrew was working less and earning more.

Though Andrew hadn't expected it when he started his business, he had more opportunities available to him ten years into his business than he would have had if he'd continued down the path of investment banking.[27]

ON LEVERAGE

This is a story I've heard dozens of times over. As they invest in entrepreneurship and become more entrepreneurial, many entrepreneurs that used to have good jobs end up financially more successful than previous peers.

They aren't pushing any harder. They're using a longer lever.

Over the past few chapters we've seen the limits of the knowledge economy and complicated knowledge work. Knowledge work, done in the Complicated domain, is no longer scarce—it's getting more and more abundant. As global education standards, communication technology, and machines increase in supply, Archimedes' lever is getting shorter and shorter. For macroeconomic reasons, jobs are getting more competitive and less profitable.

While all these factors are bad news for individuals with jobs, it's great news for entrepreneurs and people that are investing in entrepreneurship.

The improving communications technology and educational standards driving globalization and moving knowledge jobs make it easier and more inexpensive for entrepreneurs to find, hire, and manage qualified contractors and team members.

The software that's "eating jobs" is decreasing startup costs, making it easier to start a business. Entrepreneurs can outsource the non-core elements of their business and build much of their infrastructure "in the cloud" so they don't have to take out debt.

The internet has democratized distribution and production and created markets and industries that didn't exist five or ten years ago.

Entrepreneurship is more accessible, safer, and more profitable than ever before in history.

SECTION

Entrepreneurship Is Safer than Ever

In his book, *The 4-Hour Workweek*, Tim Ferriss advocates the use of negative visualizations for people considering quitting their jobs. A tradition borrowed from Stoicism, negative visualization is the practice of imagining the worst possible outcome as a way to help ourselves make difficult decisions.

What the stoics unearthed and Ferriss rediscovered was this fundamental truth: we frequently avoid making choices not because the outcome is bad, but simply because it's unknown.

Have you ever seen a cute guy or girl and wanted to go talk to them but stopped?

"Oh God, what will happen?"

Well, let's say you go introduce yourself—what is the worst that can happen?

The worst thing that's ever happened to me was: I had a girl look me up and down and laugh in my face. She laughed so hard, her spit actually hit me in the eye.

It stung. Physically because of the spit, metaphorically because of the rejection.

That pain lasted for about half an hour, and continued bothering me for a couple of weeks. Which sucks, but how bad is it really?

Does it hurt? Yes, but it's an emotional hurt. I've never seen that girl again, and no one thinks less of me because I was really bad at talking to girls when I was nineteen.

The hurt from that kind of interaction is something that humans evolved as a defense mechanism when we lived in small societies. If you lived in a tribe of fifty people and a girl rejects you, then it really did hurt. You had to see her every day. Your status was lowered in the tribe for the rest of your life; you might never find a mate, reproduce, and pass on your genes.

This principle is called loss aversion: when directly compared to each other, losses loom larger than gains.

Consider:

You are offered a gamble on the toss of a coin.

Heads, you win $150.

Tails, you lose $100.

How do you feel about it? Although the expected value is obviously positive (if you repeated the bet 100 times, you'd almost certainly come out on top), most people decline the bet.

When asked, "What is the smallest gain that you need to balance an equal chance to lose $100?", most people answer $200—twice as much as the loss.[28]

The ratio of loss aversion has been measured at between 1.5

and 2.5, meaning people typically want to see a 150–250% expected return to make the bet.

This, again, is a mentality from our evolutionary past. If a bush rustles as you trot across the African savannah and there's a 90% chance it's a delicious meal and a 10% chance that it's a hungry lion, you're better off not investigating.

You only have to be wrong once before your genes are out of the gene pool. In the modern world, in cases where death (or the career equivalent) is a real possibility, it's still a good strategy. However, that's very rarely the case.[29]

CHAPTER 5

THRIVING IN EXTREMISTAN

How Not to Be a Turkey

IT'S A MOMENT WE ARE RAISED TO DREAM OF. THAT AUNT and uncle that you haven't talked to in five years are smiling. A pair of dark spaces fragment their not-so-toothy grins. Your parents are smiling. You're wearing a medieval-styled dress with colored sashes covered in Latin characters.

You can feel the pride and excitement in the air. The promise of the future.

You ascend the raised platform and walk across the stage, deftly hiding the wince as some woman you've never met mispronounces your middle name.

You're handed a piece of paper. Years of work, tens of

thousands of dollars, capped off with an overpriced piece of paper with your name and some Latin on it.

Stepping down, you're greeted by a sign.

Most of the graduates don't realize it's already too late. Most of them are already turkeys.

The First Rule of Extremistan: Don't be a turkey.

The Second Rule of Extremistan: DO NOT BE A TURKEY.

YOU WERE RAISED IN MEDIOCRISTAN. YOU LIVE IN EXTREMISTAN.

> *"This is the central illusion in life: that randomness is risky, that it is a bad thing—and that eliminating randomness is done by eliminating randomness...Mediocristan has a lot of variations, not a single one of which is extreme; Extremistan has few variations, but those that take place are extreme."*
>
> – N.N. TALEB ANTIFRAGILE

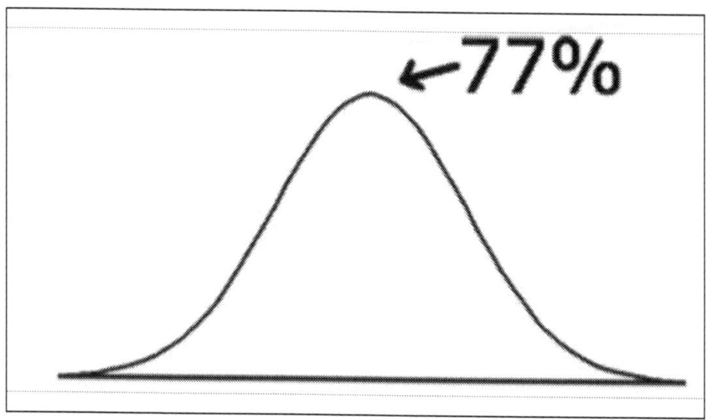

Source: 80/20 Sales and Marketing

Everyone that attended high school or college is familiar with the graph above. When the teacher wrote everyone's grades on the board, they looked like a bell curve.

A few students did really well, a few did very poorly, and most people ended up somewhere in the middle.

This is a model of the world that most people are raised to believe in: Mediocristan.

It accurately reflects how the world has operated for the vast majority of its history, and it is how the world operates for most people up until they finish school or leave a typical corporate job.

Biological systems lives in Mediocristan. If you take a hundred people and plot their heights on a graph, it will look a lot like the graph above. Most people are average height, a few are very tall, and a few are very short.

Yet the Mediocristan view of things is not how all systems work.

Non-biological systems, man-made systems, modern systems like the economy, our businesses and our careers, don't live in Mediocristan.

They live in Extremistan.

Consider how the outcomes will be distributed for those people after school.

It won't be distributed like a bell curve; it will be distributed as an 80/20 curve, also called a Pareto distribution.

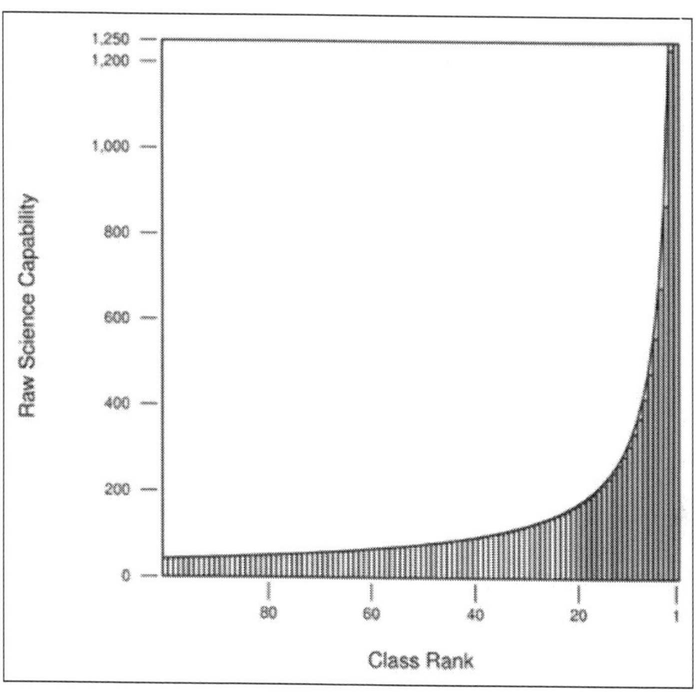

Source: 80/20 Sales and Marketing

A few students will possess the vast majority of the raw science ability. They'll get jobs at NASA or offers from well-known consulting companies. Maybe they'll get into medical school.

Many of the students that are above average, yet not exceptional, will not go to work for NASA.

The brain surgeon got A's. The guy working at the nursing home got B's.

Admittedly, this is hyperbolic, but so is reality. Think about your friends from college. Are the outcomes "fairly" distributed? Or are a few doing exceptionally well, and the majority struggling?

Everything about our existence up until we graduate from college (and much later, for people that get jobs afterwards) confirms the illusion that we are living in Mediocristan.

The school system is set up to enforce the belief that we live in a world which is safe and predictable.

This Gaussian bell curve distribution makes sense intuitively to us. It's *fair* (a dangerous concept).

We make a lot of our life decisions under the belief that we are living in Mediocristan. But we are not.

Many people have doubled (or lost all of) their net worth in a single moment: a company goes public or announces bankruptcy. A stock quintuples or crashes.

Vast, man-made empires have been toppled by a single event—the storming of the Bastille, the signing of The Declaration of Independence. These individual events are what change looks like in Extremistan.

Sudden, violent, and unforeseen.

As technology continues to evolve, we are increasingly living our lives in Extremistan. As more and more of the world around us goes from biological to man-made, the degree to which our careers and lives are lived in Extremistan is increasing.

As technology and globalization continue to advance, the Middle Class is dying.

THE ZUCKERBERG PHENOMENON

Just as you're being thrown from Mediocristan to Extremistan as you come of age, there is also a global, structural change towards Extremistan. Not only were the twenty-year-olds entering the workforce a hundred years ago less sheltered, they were entering a world that was much more like Mediocristan than the world we live in now.

When parents, CEOs, and college administrators make projections of safety, it's not done out of deception. It's an honest belief based on their life experiences. Life experiences that, for the most part, took place in Mediocristan. Many of our parents did spend their entire careers at one company, living in one house. That was a reality for much of the 20th century.

As technology has improved and the world becomes more centralized, Extremistan is replacing Mediocristan and the effects are more extreme. Bill Gates was the youngest billionaire at 31. Then Zuckerberg did it at 23.

The wealth gap is increasing. There were fewer wars in the 20th century than any preceding century, but significantly more people were killed in those wars than in previous ones. Those are symptoms of living in Extremistan.

Things have been very peaceful for our generation compared with past generations, but the power to do massive damage is now in the hands of individuals more so than at any previous point in history. One nuclear bomb in an extremist's hands can cause more harm to the world compared to any weapon available before it.

The same phenomenon is true of corporations and the reality of long-term, stable jobs for our generation. Just as the world appears more peaceful now than it's ever been, we're at the level where more people than ever in history (mistakenly) believe stable, full-time jobs will be broadly available for the next fifty years. They have been available for the past fifty years, so why wouldn't that continue?

Just as we assume peaceful circumstances today means peace will continue, we assume the same will be true of employment.

We assume jobs are safe because they've always been safe, not because there's good evidence they will be in the future.

HOW TO BE A TURKEY

Coming out of college or out of a traditional corporate job, most people think like turkeys. I thought like a turkey.

It's based on our understanding of the world having spent

our entire lives in Mediocristan, a turkey's world. Up until relatively recent history, it's been highly rational.

It's also wrong.

> *"A turkey is fed for a thousand days by a butcher; every day confirms to its staff of analysts that butchers love turkeys 'with increased statistical confidence.' The butcher will keep feeding the turkey until a few days before Thanksgiving... [The] turkey will have a revision of belief—right when its confidence in the statement that the butcher loves turkeys is maximal and 'it is very quiet' and soothingly predictable in the life of the turkey."*
>
> – N.N. TALEB

The most obvious example of a world where a single, irreversible decision dictates the future is that of a turkey before Thanksgiving.

From the day a Thanksgiving turkey is born, everything about its life indicates that things are only going to get better. It's hatched in a safe, sterile environment. It's cared for and fed daily.

Every single day, this pattern happens again. It wakes up to find plenty of food and a place to live.

It is at the moment when the turkey has the most historical data to show that its life is likely to keep improving, on the 4th Wednesday of November, that it realizes—it's not so good to be a turkey.

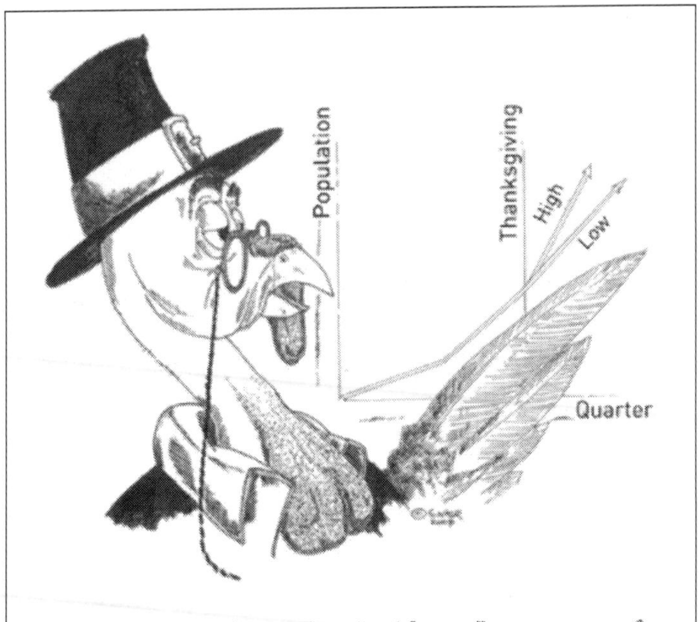

FIGURE 4. A turkey using "evidence"; unaware of Thanksgiving, it is making "rigorous" future projections based on the past. Credit: George Nasr

Source: Antifragile – Nassim Taleb

That is, the moment when we are most confident about our security is the moment in which we are in fact most likely to be endangered.

It's already too late though. The turkey, fattened and slothful, is out of options.

Don't be a Turkey.

HOW SAFE IS IT TO BE AN ACCOUNTANT?

Let's say you're an accountant that's worked at a large firm for a few years. You have the option to leave and start a company, or take an apprenticeship at a smaller company that may or may not succeed.

The way most people would typically look at that situation is: you could leave something safe to pursue something risky. You would have to be particularly passionate or particularly excited to do that, wouldn't you?

If we lived in Mediocristan, that would be an accurate thing to say.

If we lived in Extremistan (and we do), that would be incorrect.

Let's look at why by comparing two individuals with real stories. One we'll call Rand; the other, Max.

Rand had a steady job as an accountant, but left to start his own company. Max stayed at the current company and continued to work as an accountant because he felt it was the smart, responsible, and safe thing to do. Everything in his life, the lives of his parents, and the lives of his friends up to that point indicated that this choice was smart.

Max continues putting in his hours, forty per week in the slow months and eighty plus leading up to tax season. He's arranging spreadsheets and getting paid. The $2,876 check hits his bank account every two weeks, just like a butcher filling the turkey's trough.

Steady income creates a Mediocristan illusion of steady value creation. This is dangerous. Fatally dangerous. It's allowing us to accumulate silent risk.

It is entirely possible to generate income without creating value for the world, or creating dramatically less value than you're being compensated for. See: every government bureaucracy ever. Or, more specifically, see Max.

Max believes he's doing something valuable until, one day, he gets a letter from the Human Resources department.

> *Dear Max,*
>
> *Your position has been replaced by Marissa. Marissa lives in the Philippines and has a degree from a London University and is more than happy to earn $10 an hour doing the exact same work that you're doing.*
>
> *Best Regards,*
>
> *Human Resources*

Any non-biological system in Extremistan without variation is accumulating silent risk, and one example of that, Max just discovered, was his career.

The longer the market goes without having a correction, the

larger the correction will be when it happens. The longer we go in our careers and businesses without variation or randomness, the larger the amount of underlying risk we accumulate.

Because he's been shielded from the Extremistan reality for so long, Max made decisions based on his belief in Mediocristan. He has a mortgage, a family to support, and expensive spending habits.

These are also silent risks. If he loses his job as an accountant, he hasn't built up a skillset around building systems as opposed to operating within existing systems—he's used to following orders, which dramatically reduces the options available to him.

He also has more monthly expenses. Because he believed that his steady paycheck would continue coming and growing over time, he's made life decisions (like taking out a mortgage) based on that.

Maybe there is a good opportunity for him in another city; but how can he move when he has a mortgage?

Because the silent risk has been accumulating for decades, it all hits him at once. He could lose his house, put an enormous amount of stress on his family, and have to dramatically reduce his lifestyle expenses.

Moderate amounts of volatility are healthy. Lying on the ground and having a trainer drop a ten pound medicine ball on you, you catching it, and throwing it back to them will make you stronger.

Large amounts of volatility, like having a car dropped on you, will kill you.

Likewise, moderate amounts of volatility in our careers and businesses are healthy. It's the large events, the butcher's hatchet, that kill us.

If you put yourself in a position which creates very little value in the market for ten years, and it gets replaced by machines or Marissa from the Phillipines when you're 40 years old, at peak earning potential, with a family and mortgage, you're a Turkey on Thanksgiving.

THRIVING IN EXTREMISTAN: HOW NOT TO BE A TURKEY

Now let's talk to Rand. Rand used to work at the desk next to Max.

Rand left his job as an accountant, for reasons that most people leave their jobs: to start companies or join smaller, more entrepreneurial companies. He decided that he didn't want to spend the next 25 years of his life working in a position he didn't enjoy and didn't find meaningful or fulfilling. He certainly didn't think it was smart at the time, but it's worth evaluating that again in light of the Turkey Problem.

Rand spent six months hiking the Appalachian Trail, and then he bought an around-the-world plane ticket. On his trips, it was often very hard for him to find healthy food. There wasn't anything that had all the nutrition of a full meal, so he decided to start a company making meal replacement bars.

Rand isn't making a lot of money right now.

He's baking the meal replacement bars at home while living in his parents' basement.

The difference is that for Rand, not making money is feedback. There's no silent risk accumulating.

If Rand puts up a website and no one buys his bars, that's feedback. He can adjust and has adjusted. Money wasn't hitting his bank account, so he's changed the product; he's changed the marketing; sales are starting to improve.

Rand has to go out and peck for his food. It's not just showing up in the trough. He doesn't get a steady paycheck. But now he's learning where to forage, how to forage, and the days he goes hungry are the days he's learning the most.

Entrepreneurship is certainly not without risk. Issues of personal debt, damaged relationships, and lost earning potential can and usually will always arise. There are, however, differences in how it deals with risk.

The first is that entrepreneurial risk is more visible than the silent risk accumulated by people in most jobs. If Rand's sales decline this month, he knows right away and starts to adjust. If Max's company starts to do poorly or his role is about to be outsourced, the CEO will send out a comforting memo that everything is just about to turn around and will be fine. There's no feedback until Max gets the final letter from human resources.

If you do an accounting role which creates no value, but keep getting a paycheck for ten years, and then the HR department sends you a letter and Marissa from the Philippines takes your job, you have very few options. Your professional network is based around an industry that is being moved overseas. Your skillset is based around operating in a predefined system rather than one you can define for yourself.

Rand, on the other hand, has a much bumpier-looking income. Some months he does well and some months he does not. But it's getting better, and he's gaining skills. He's building a network of other entrepreneurs that can help him in the future. He's creating the systems and changing them when they aren't producing the results he wants.

Beyond the risk being more visible and the feedback mechanisms more direct, Rand also develops another skillset in the complex domain: *dealing* with risk.

It is in seeking a path with no risk, no mistakes, and no variation (stable income, clear promotion path) that Max has in fact exposed himself to a massive downside—getting fired at forty without a skillset for creating new systems or operating in complex environments, the metaphorical car falling on his head.

This is not because Max is stupid or Rand is smart. Everything about Max's environment—his time in school, his parents' career, and his own career up until this point—has confirmed the fact that his path was smart and safe.

The rules and the leverage points have changed in ways that were never made clear to us growing up. Many people are entering Thanksgiving week.

RISK LIVES IN THE FUTURE

> *"Artisans, say, taxi drivers, prostitutes (a very, very old profession), carpenters, plumbers, tailors, and dentists, have some volatility in their income but they are rather robust to a minor professional Black Swan, one that would bring their income to a complete halt. Their risks are visible. Not so with employees, who have no volatility, but can be surprised to see their income going to zero after a phone call from the personnel department. Employees' risks are hidden. Thanks to variability, these artisanal careers harbor a bit of antifragility: small variations make them adapt and change continuously by learning from the environment and being, sort of, continuously under pressure to be fit."*
>
> – N. N. TALEB

Many of us have been fed the belief that traditional careers are safe and that they have *always* been safe. It's what I believed for a long time, and if we look at historical trends, it makes sense.

The trouble with historical is exactly that—it's historical.

Saying a career that's been safe for the last forty years will be safe for the next forty is like saying that the 20th century was less violent than the 19th century.

If you exclude the two World Wars, it's true—it was the safest, least violent century in history.

However, in Extremistan, risk doesn't live in the past; it lives in the future. It's the one event that comes once in a lifetime and defines Extremistan, so saying it hasn't happened in our lifetimes is exactly the point. It's coming.

It only takes one massive World War to make an entire century the most violent in history. Never before in human history has one nation had the power to destroy 99% of humanity with the push of a button, but that's a reality we've been living with since the Cold War, and despite all efforts made at disarmament, it's one we will continue to live with.

Albeit undesirable, it's reality. The world is coming more and more to resemble Extremistan every *day*, and you have to realize that so you can adjust accordingly.

The fact that Max's decision has been safe for the last one hundred years is in no way indicative that it's going to be safe in the future.

I don't say all this to scare. I say it to make you aware.

What was once safe is now risky. What was once risky is now safe.

SECTION

The Long Tail

How Entrepreneurs with Second Rate Degrees Are Getting Rich

The Long Tail, a concept popularized by *Wired* editor Chris Anderson in his book by the same name, explains that because of technology, primarily the internet, the traditional rules around business and entrepreneurship have changed.

In 1998, Derek Sivers was a musician living in New York. In his words, he'd "already made it." He had bought a house from his music and was living his childhood dream of being a musician. He thought it might be cool if he could take his music and sell it to people over this thing called "the internet." He spent three months building a website, getting a payment processor and shopping cart set-up, and eventually managed to actually sell some of his CDs.

When his friends heard he could sell his CDs online, they asked him if he would sell their CDs online. Derek's a pretty nice guy, so he said: "Why not?" Then *their* friends asked. So Derek started charging musicians to post their CDs and turned his hobby into **CDBaby.com**.

CD Baby was eventually acquired by Amazon for $22 million. CD Baby's success was because it was one of the first companies built around the concept of the Long Tail. It leveraged the internet to make it possible to sell CDs for independent musicians who, in the past, had never been able to get their record into record stores.

This was revolutionary for the music industry. Derek described it as though he were in the 60's at Woodstock: "Woah man, the shackles are off! Those record labels can't hold us back anymore." [30]

In a world where distribution is controlled by record stores and the costs of holding inventory are non-trivial, there's a cutoff point where it stops making sense for the record stores to stock shelves with your CD. A record store has to pay for more shelf space, so if a record doesn't sell a certain number of copies, then they can't afford to stock your CD.

Because CD Baby was selling online, the cost of holding more inventory, of listing more CDs for sale, rapidly approached zero. Once they'd built the website, the cost of adding another product page was negligible and decreased with each product.

If you wanted to get your CD sold by a traditional distributor, you had to pay a few thousand dollars to get it set up. It took nine months or more to get paid because the artist wasn't paid until the stores had returned any albums that didn't sell. You didn't know who your customers were, so you couldn't market or sell future albums to them.

To sell with CD Baby, it cost $35 to set your CD up on the site. You were paid every week and you were given a list of your customers, including their email addresses, in order to sell to them.

These aren't marginal changes, they're order of magnitude changes.

Cost: ~$3000 → $35 = ~100 times cheaper

Time to get paid: 9 months → 1 week = ~36 times faster

Customer Communication: None → You own every customer's contact info

CD Baby revolutionized the music industry by escaping the limitations of the short head and "revealing" the Long Tail.

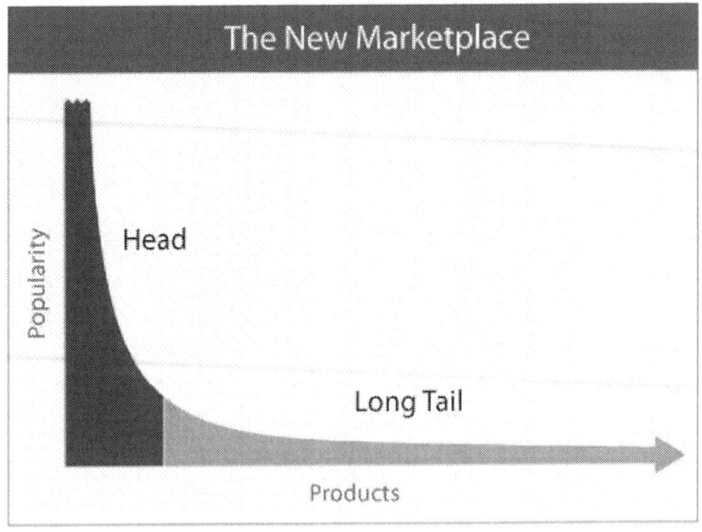

In *The Long Tail*, Anderson recounts the story of a friend whose band, Birdmonster, saw the benefits of the Long Tail made possible in part by Derek and CD Baby.

For bands looking to get started, there's no way around hustling for gigs. While most bands are forced into pestering club owners for gigs, Birdmonster searched for clubs that had already booked headliners but still had "TBA" for the opening band. Using Google, they would search for and contact those clubs. They used the direct relationship they had created with their fans over email to encourage them to follow their popular Myspace page, and then used that page as a way to show club owners they had fans who would come to the show, making it easier to get gigs.

Once they had a good record of live gigs and a stable fan base, Birdmonster recorded three tracks in a local independent music studio and then used inexpensive software on their personal computers—the kind that a decade earlier was only available commercially—to edit the music and list their album on CD Baby.

CD Baby made the album available for sale online, where it could be bought or streamed just like any musician from a major label.

They emailed the song tracks to a handful of blogs, who reviewed the album and drove more fans to the band. As they started getting press, managers, labels, and industry insiders started calling them for deals.

Birdmonster turned them down.

A music label exists for four main reasons: talent scouring, financing to rent a studio (like startup capital for a business), distribution, and marketing.

From Birdmonster's angle, they could do all those things themselves, but better and cheaper.

They already knew they were talented since they'd been getting gigs. Since they could edit the music on their own computers, they didn't need financing to rent a studio. CD Baby provided distribution to all the top services like iTunes and Rhapsody, and weekly payouts instead of payout nine months later like traditional record distributors. The effect of their Myspace page (it was the early 2000's) and a personal email to well known blogs was greater than anything record labels could provide in terms of marketing.

What Birdmonster's story shows about the music industry, the internet has done for entrepreneurs at large. We're now seeing the Long Tail phenomenon come to businesses as a whole. Just as technology made it viable for small bands to sell their records online, it's also made entrepreneurship more accessible than ever.

THE LONG TAIL OR WHAT'S MAKING ENTREPRENEURSHIP MORE ACCESSIBLE

Just like scientists sequencing the human genome were unable to predict how fast technology would enable the project to accelerate, the same has occurred with the technology needed to start a business. The barriers to entry have come down dramatically faster than most people have realized.

There are three primary forces of the Long Tail which have driven this shift making entrepreneurship more accessible than ever.

1. **The Democratization of the Tools of Production: Product Creation Costs Are Decreasing**—Just as cheap software let Birdmonster produce music from their laptops, cheap tools have allowed entrepreneurs to start and run a business from anywhere with little to no capital up front.

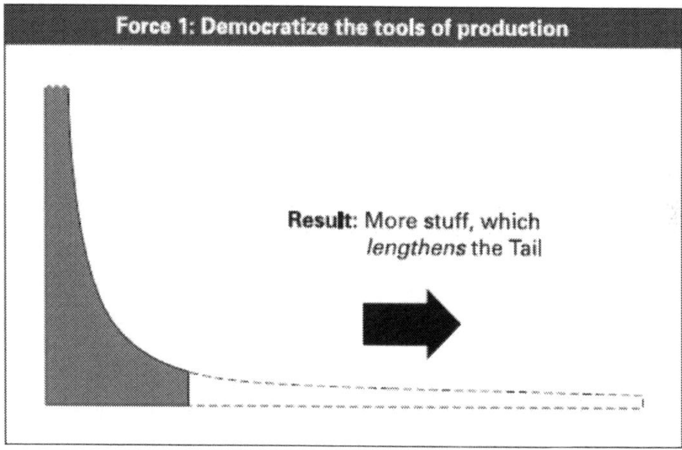

Source: The Long Tail – Chris Anderson

2. **Democratization of Distribution: Everyone Is a Media Company**—It's easier and cheaper than ever to reach those markets. Thanks to digital distribution like Youtube, podcasting, and blogging, the newly revealed markets are easier to reach and market to than ever.

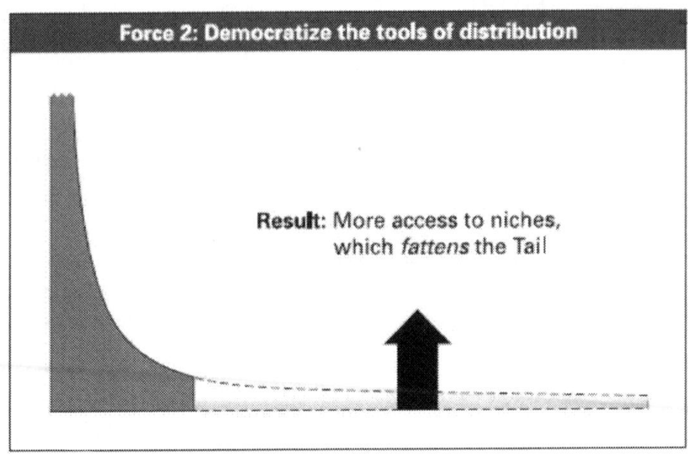

Source: The Long Tail – Chris Anderson

3. **New Markets Are Revealed Every Day**—There are more new markets willing to buy those things. In all markets there are more niches than major players. Just as a record store could only stock so many records, traditional retail markets could only support so many businesses. The internet has changed the rules, revealing new markets and businesses every day.

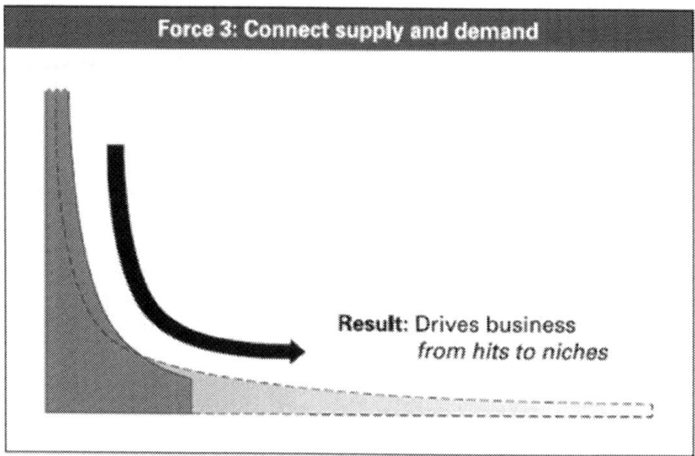

Source: The Long Tail – Chris Anderson

In short, the internet had made it possible to start a business just by being clever and ambitious. If you wanted to open a retail store twenty years ago, you had to buy a lease on Main St., which meant either coming from a family that had that money or convincing a bank to give it to you. Now fast forward to 2015 and there's a new kind of real estate company: Google.

If you can make the best site, you can get the best "real estate." So if you can figure out what "best site" means, you can have similarly powerful real estate as someone on Main St. did two decades ago.

There are more markets that are getting bigger, and they're easier to reach. The Long Tail is getting fatter, longer, and more accessible.

The 7 Day Startup, a self-published book by Dan Norris, teaches entrepreneurs how to identify, build, and test startup ideas in a week.

The book, which Dan originally planned to give away for free on his website as a PDF, shot to the top of the Amazon Best Seller list for Startups and has sold tens of thousands of copies less than a year after being released—a feat few books achieve in their lifetimes.

Why was the book so popular?

The 7 Day Startup lays out a very simple, step-by-step plan for how to launch a business in seven days.

The book is based on Dan's experiences having launched and failed at over a half dozen businesses. If you aren't an experienced entrepreneur, you're making a lot of assumptions when you get started.

This had always been the case. Inexperienced entrepreneurs had always made lots of assumptions and frequently lost lots of money. Experienced entrepreneurs had always developed better gut instincts.

What's different *now* is that you can launch a business in seven days for less than a few hundred bucks and grow it into a real, valuable asset.

Dan's own business, WP Curve, which provides Wordpress support for small businesses, is the case study. Dan launched the business in seven days and is on track to hit high six figures in revenue within two years of getting it off the ground.[31]

What's changed in the last ten years, since we started shifting out of the Knowledge economy and into the Entrepreneurial economy, and how has Dan taken advantage of it?

The Three Factors of the Long Tail:

1. The Democratization of the Tools of Production

2. The Democratization of Distribution

3. New Markets Are Revealed Every Day

Let's break those down further.

CHAPTER 6

THE DEMOCRATIZATION OF THE TOOLS OF PRODUCTION

Product Creation Costs Are Decreasing

MANY PEOPLE OBJECT TO STARTING A BUSINESS BECAUSE it's perceived as being expensive, or requiring a lot of capital up front. Would-be entrepreneurs imagine having to go out and buy a lot of physical equipment, hire staff, and rent office space. For a large and growing number of businesses, that's no longer the case.

The Social Network, the movie chronicling Facebook's rise to a multi-billion dollar company, depicts Mark Zuckerberg starting Facebook in his college dorm room. Basecamp, a multi-million dollar project management software company, was started by Jason Fried and David Heinemeier Hansson, while living in different countries and while also running a web development consultancy.

But it's not just tech companies.

RENT TO OWN: THE SHARING ECONOMY

Over the last decade, a more publicly available internet has enabled the "Sharing Economy," which has democratized the tools of production. Technology and the internet have brought trust and transparency to markets, which lets people share existing resources and repurpose them into higher and better uses to take them from a lower to a higher area of productivity. The sharing economy has made manufacturing more efficient—you can create increased inventory without immediately needing more supply. We saw the implications of this with CD Baby: it's gotten dramatically cheaper—as much as one hundred times cheaper—to invest in entrepreneurship than it was a decade ago.

Let's use the hotel industry as an example.

In the past, if there weren't enough rooms in a city for visitors, Hilton went and built a new hotel. They would pay millions of dollars for a piece of land downtown, millions of dollars to construct a hotel, and then millions of dollars to hire staff to run it.

The sharing economy version of that is a company called AirBnB, which allows homeowners to post their rooms online so people coming to visit can stay in them. It's often less expensive than a hotel and many people like getting to know a city as a resident instead of as a tourist.

Let's say Julian has a house that he owns in Dallas, Texas. He usually has one spare bedroom, so he lists it on AirBnB as available.

He has filled a market need that ten years ago would have only been available to someone with millions of dollars that could build a hotel. A market opportunity that would have been available to a few thousand people that could afford to build a hotel is now available to a few million people that may have a spare bedroom.

There are not many more houses now in the U.S. than there were 5 years ago, but AirBnB has created more inventory (extra rooms to stay in) without creating more supply (building hotels).

Uber and Lyft have done for the taxi industry what AirBnB has done for the hotel industry—anyone with a car can become a taxi driver by signing up online to drive for the service. In the past it was difficult and expensive to become a taxi driver. Some cities require drivers to invest tens of thousands of dollars to buy a medallion just to drive a taxi.

Uber and Lyft now let anyone do the work by instead going through a background check. A lot of people use this as supplemental income when making a job transition. They don't have to invest thousands of dollars—they can just sign up on the website and make a few thousand bucks a month between jobs.

Others like Digital Ocean, a hosting company, have done the same thing with digital real estate by enabling cloud based development. In the past, if you wanted to build a software product or host your website, you had to go buy a big physical computer server to sit in your office. Digital Ocean, and other similar companies, let developers deploy an SSD cloud server in less than a minute at one of their server farms. If you only need a small amount of server space, you don't have to go buy a server—you can rent or share a section of one.

Broadly this has had the same effect for entrepreneurs that CD Baby had for musicians. The cost of the tools needed to invest in entrepreneurship has dropped dramatically because the infrastructure has gotten so much more efficient. Let's look at a few of the primary tools and how entrepreneurs are using them.

SOFTWARE AS A SERVICE (SAAS): PLUG AND PLAY TOOLS AND SYSTEMS

Software as a service has arisen primarily in the last decade and facilitates a large part of the sharing economy. Instead of having to buy expensive equipment or sign long-term contracts, entrepreneurs can buy month-to-month access to different services that they need.

Previously, a new company would have had to buy accounting

software that would cost hundreds of dollars. Now, instead of buying expensive accounting software, you can use a month-to-month service like Xero, which starts at $9 a month.

Dan Norris of WP Curve runs his entire business using around $1,200 in subscriptions to software services each month. Not a nominal cost, but considering he can administer a 35-person team across five continents for less than the lease of a typical storefront, it's pretty amazing.

Instead of spending tens of thousands of dollars for a two-year lease, you can set up a website using Shopify for $14/month.

In some cases, these services are even free. Microsoft Office cost around $200 in 2008. Google Documents, a cloud based version that fills the same need as Microsoft Office, is completely free.

Those are three specific examples, but this is true for all the different tools required to start a business. The advantages are profound:

1. Dramatic reduction in risk and cost—you're often paying just 1% of the cost to get started compared to ten years ago.

2. Dramatic increase in potential—because you can only buy as much as you need, you can buy best-in-class software.

Venture capitalist Ben Horowitz, the CEO of the first cloud computing company, Loudcloud, said his customers were paying approximately $150,000 a month in 2000 to run a basic internet application. Running that same application today in Amazon's cloud costs about $1,500 a month.

If the same decrease had happened to cars and homes, a $50,000 luxury car would cost $500 today and a half million dollar home would cost $5,000.

Because technology develops faster than biological systems (like our brains), we're not very good at understanding these kind of changes, but they happen all the time in the modern world. For individuals fixated on jobs and trying to operate in the Complicated domain, these are tremendous threats to their career security. For entrepreneurs operating the complex domain, they're opportunities to be taken advantage of.

MARKETPLACES AND CONTRACTORS: PLUG AND PLAY TEAM MEMBERS AND PROJECT PARTNERS

As SaaS companies simplify access to the tools and infrastructure for entrepreneurs, hiring platforms have shifted hiring from a geographically local activity to an international one.

Imagine you've always loved craft beer and want to start an online publication about craft beer. Instead of hiring an editor on a full-time salary and hoping the new business worked, you could start working with someone on a part-time basis and pay them for a few hours of work each week.

If the business started to take off, great! If it doesn't, you haven't started paying health insurance and gone through the expensive process of setting up a full time team member.

Again, we see the same pattern as with Software as a Service:

1. Dramatic reduction in cost and risk—less expensive and easier to find, lower risk

2. Dramatic increase in potential—find the best qualified person in the world

Previously, finding an editor for a craft beer magazine would have meant posting up job applications locally and hoping to find an expert. Now, it means you can find the most qualified person on the planet.

Platforms like UpWork allow previous employers to leave reviews on team members and for people to build portfolios of work. Just as Amazon took a traditional retail shelf and added online reviews making the buying process easier, online marketplaces make the hiring process easier.

Instead of a large, up-front investment in hiring and training someone who may or may not be good enough for the role, you're able to make a small investment, over time, in someone that has been vetted by other people in your industry.

SELF-EDUCATION: INFORMATION WANTS TO BE FREE

In 1984, at the first Hackers Conference, Whole Earth Catalog founder Stewart Brand was overheard telling Apple co-founder Steve Wozniak the now iconic phrase: *"Information wants to be free."*

The internet has done more to facilitate information transparency than any technology since the printing press. Knowledge that used to be opaque and hard to source is often now just a Google search away.

Scott Young, a young entrepreneur who now teaches others about advanced learning strategies, put himself through the entire MIT course material in twelve months for two thousand dollars.

He bought the textbooks and was able to get all the classes online. This education at MIT would have cost around $150,000 and four years of his life. Instead, he was able to put himself through the entire course material in twelve months for $2,000. That's around 98.7% cheaper than the cost of a degree from MIT, not including the three years he saved.

Jesse Lawler, who runs the development firm in Vietnam, taught himself to code iPhone apps using free or cheap classes online. In a world without the internet, where information was expensive and the only way to learn was to get a degree, that made sense. In a world with the internet, where information is rapidly approaching free, it's hard to rationalize spending money paying for access to general knowledge when you can get the same knowledge for free.

It's also worth noting that Scott put himself through MIT, not

Spokane Community College. He put himself through one of the premier universities on Earth for around the cost of a single class at a local community college.

The same pattern emerges:

1. Dramatic reduction in cost and risk—cheaper and easier to get the knowledge you need

2. Dramatic increase in potential—learn from the most qualified people on Earth

Fifty years ago, every time you wanted to look up a specific medical study, you had to go to a university library, find the reference book you were looking for, pull it off the shelf, and try and decode the scientific text. If someone was that interested, they might as well just go to medical school.

The same is true of the marketable skills it takes to run a business. The tools of learning and production were made difficult to access for the average person in the past.

Companies like Udemy and Team TreeHouse, which host online courses, have given people access to more valuable resources than universities at a fraction of the cost. The same phenomenon that Scott Young created for himself is now being created by companies making it even more accessible.

Online forums and communities in your industry let you learn from other people in the trenches day-to-day. No one is going to sell enough copies of a book about User Onboarding for web applications or marketing iPhone Apps to stock it in a bookstore or offer it in a university, but those work on the internet. The Long Tail has let businesses emerge that are hyper specific and couldn't have existed in a retail world, a concept we'll come back to in the next chapter.

IT'S CHEAPER TO MAKE WIDGETS! (AND USEFUL STUFF TOO)

The advantages of the Sharing Economy extend not just to the infrastructure required to run a business and digital products, but to the democratized production of physical products as well.

Twenty years ago, most small physical product businesses were limited to manufacturing in the U.S.

Manufacturing overseas was simply too difficult. You had to use large order quantities, and you had to have connections. If you wanted to manufacture in China, you needed to have hundreds of thousands in capital to invest, *and* you needed to have a background in manufacturing in China to know the right people.

Imagine, in the year 2000, you had a product idea. You had to fly to China. You had to walk the streets and talk to the factory brokers—middlemen that made the process more expensive and inefficient—instead of talking straight to the owner. You were likely to make a lot of expensive mistakes before you even got the manufacturing process started. Once you *did* get it started, you were going to have to put down a hefty payment for the first run.

That's no longer the scenario that entrepreneurs face when they want to make products in China. Now you can source on Alibaba, a Chinese site where factories list all the products they manufacture. They have their own websites, so you can choose from thousands of options and find the one or two factories that have a track record doing projects similar to what you're looking for.

Jimmy and Doug from Minaal wanted to make a stylish travel bag specifically for entrepreneurs, something that was both practical and would look good in a board room. They were able to find one of the best bag factories in the world, have their prototypes made for free, and then pre-sell the product using Kickstarter, a crowdfunding platform.

Ten years ago, companies that sold products in the U.S. would never announce who their suppliers were overseas for fear that competitors would use them. That's starting to break down. Most suppliers are listed on the internet on sites like **Alibaba.com** and are easy to find.

The other major drive facilitating physical product manufacturing has been advances in communication technology and education. To even know who the main players were, much less actually place an order, required getting on a plane and working connections on the ground in China. Ten years ago, we were on the tail end of the fax age, so even if you were able to do business without visiting it meant faxing back and forth product design templates and reviewing them on the phone. Now, you can share your screen with someone on a free Skype call.

Language proficiency was much worse in China as well. As education has gotten better, it's much easier to communicate with a factory. Even if a Chinese factory could have put up a website, they may not have anyone that could actually communicate with English speakers.

Getting feedback on early prototypes, a process that would have required a translator and a plane flight before, now requires you to send a representational model (which you can hire a contractor to make using relatively cheap software) via a PDF email attachment; have them open it on their end; and call over Skype to discuss it.

Even in physical product manufacturing, we see the same trend:

1. Dramatic reduction in cost and risk—cheaper and easier to find a factory, develop a prototype, and get it manufactured.

2. Dramatic increase in potential—find the best factory in the world for your product.

It's dramatically cheaper and easier to produce better products, but how will you market them? How do you reach customers?

CHAPTER 7

THE DEMOCRATIZATION OF DISTRIBUTION

EVERYONE HAS A SMART PHONE NOW.

That sounds blasé. Let's try again.

Everyone has a computer in their pocket.

Still blasé?

Everyone has access to the sum total of human knowledge and resources at their fingertips, 24 hours a day, 7 days a week, 365 days a year.

Getting closer.

The punchline is this: the gatekeepers are dying. You, sitting in your apartment, can communicate with everyone on Earth more effectively than any media company twenty years ago.

The internet has made distribution and the ability to reach people possible now in industries where it wasn't even a pipe dream before. Even though there were good bands before CD Baby, they didn't have any way to get their music out to people without getting permission from record company executives.

There were lots of people that could have been entrepreneurs ten years ago, but didn't have a way to reach the market. If you talk to any experienced entrepreneur, they will almost always tell you that the biggest challenge a new business faces is sales and marketing.

That meant if you wanted to start a business selling portable bars, like the one I worked with, you had to:

1. Get them manufactured in the U.S., because there was no way you were manufacturing in China twenty years ago as a small business.

2. Be in the industry, or you had to have spent years on the ground making connections with existing distributors.

Now, you just need to rank #1 on Google.

That's not easy, per se, but it's a heck of a lot easier and less expensive than spending two years going to trade shows every weekend.

Being able to use the internet to reach consumers directly is also a better value. If you go to a trade show every year and have inefficient manufacturing processes, you pass those costs along to consumers. It can cost thousands of dollars more to manufacture a single product in the U.S. than in other countries, and tens of thousands of dollars to attend a single trade show—costs that are eventually passed along in the final price.

By manufacturing in China and distributing directly to consumers over the internet, we were able to reduce the cost of the bars by around 25%, and improve the quality of the product.

FROM THREE CHANNELS TO THREE BILLION

In the early days of television, access to viewers' attention was owned by a small handful of major corporations like CBS and ABC. Choices were limited to *60 Minutes* and *The Wide World of Sports*. A small handful of companies earned all the money.

Then cable came along and companies like HBO, CNN, and ESPN appeared. Distribution became easier, but there was still a relatively small number of options.

Then broadband internet arrived, and the floodgates opened.

With the creation of Youtube, everyone has access to media distribution.

Mike and Kimberly, two early readers of this book, alerted me to the creation of the game walkthrough market, also known as "Let's Players," because the videos originally boasted titles like "Let's Play *Legend of Zelda*." Using $20 screen recorder software, a $30 webcam, and a $60 microphone, Let's Players play video games and offer commentary to prospective gamers. PewDiePie, a Swedish Let's Player, has generated $12 million dollars from his videos.

The Oculus Rift Virtual Reality headset first sent its market feelers out through Let's Players, who tested out games with the headset. Now the headset is rapidly on its way to being commonly available to the masses.

As more and more platforms are built, there are more and more distribution channels opening up every day. Youtube, iTunes, and Google are just the well-known examples.

Blogging has seen the same transition. Blogs with a single author now receive more traffic than many traditional newspapers. Dan Norris's blog on **WPCurve.com** lets him reach tens of thousands of people for free each month, who then become aware of his paid service.

You are a media company. What traditionally cost hundreds of thousands in advertising is now available to you.

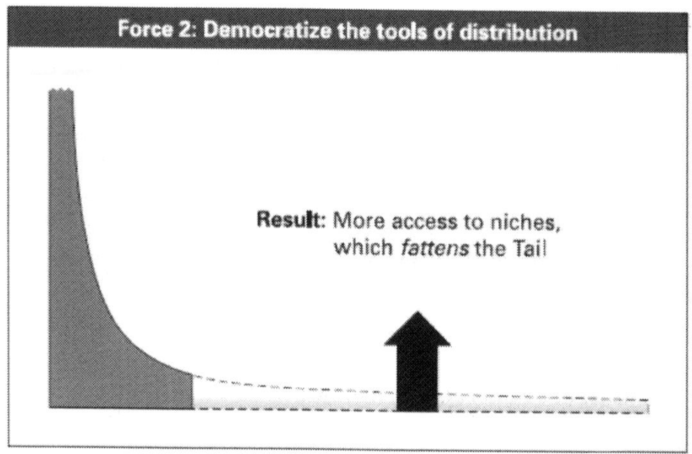

Source: The Long Tail – Chris Anderson

The democratization of distribution has fattened all the tails. Products have gotten cheaper to make and markets have gotten easier to reach, but are there enough markets to support this shift?

CHAPTER 8

NEW MARKETS ARE CREATED EVERY DAY

BECAUSE OF THE NATURE OF TRADITIONAL RETAIL, markets which weren't in the head of the Long Tail were never commercially viable. If you couldn't sell enough records within a ten mile radius of the record store in downtown Boise, you weren't going to get distribution from a major label.

One of the examples Derek Sivers cited as a successful musician on CD Baby was a woman that sailed around the world and made music exclusively for sailors. She was the best in the world at recording songs for that very niche audience.

There have always been sailors, but not until the internet was it possible to reach them in a cost-effective way. Selling a few thousand CDs a month for a record company that had tens of thousands of dollars in overhead is a flop, but for an independent artist, it's a full-time living.[32]

The same is true of businesses.

If you look at sales in any market, it typically follows a power law distribution like the head to tail curve we saw earlier. If we plot the same curve on a logarithmic scale, where each step is a factor of ten ($1, $10, $100, $1000, etc), then it should form a straight line as in the graph below.

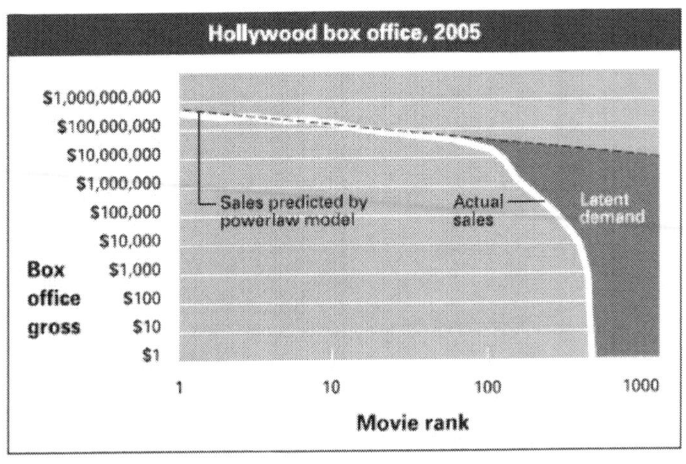

Source: The Long Tail – Chris Anderson

In this example from Chris Anderson's *The Long Tail*, actual sales don't follow the dotted line. Traditionally in movies, just as in music, if you aren't making it into major distribution (in this case movie theaters), you aren't making any money. After the top one hundred, we see movies that only got a little bit of regional distribution as the curve drops off, and then it falls to zero at around the five hundred rank for movies that got no distribution.

What *should* look like the Long Tail graph we saw earlier actually looks like this:

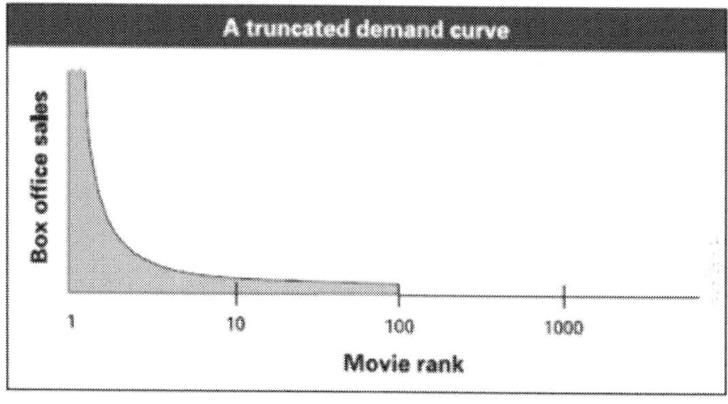

Source: The Long Tail – Chris Anderson

Because movie theatres, record stores, and retail businesses can't serve the area labeled latent demand.

The latent demand has always existed. There was always a demand for music from small independent artists before CD Baby, but the economics of retail didn't allow it. There was always a market for niche movies before Netflix, but the market didn't allow it. There are also demands for an enormous number of products and services that weren't possible in the past.

Why is it possible now?

THE INTERNET = GEOGRAPHY IS IRRELEVANT = MILLIONS OF NEW MARKET VERTICALS

Let's look at how law firms work now versus how they are changing and will work in the future.

Right now you have a local lawyer who you do business with because he's geographically close to you, but he probably doesn't have a deep understanding of your business model or industry.

If you were able to work with a lawyer that intimately understood the needs of your business, it would be better for both the lawyer and you.

You wouldn't have to pay for the lawyer to educate himself on the details of your industry and business. The lawyer would be able to give a better product at a better price.

An online marketplace like UpCounsel will let you find a lawyer with specialized skills who is an exact fit for what you need. Say you needed to find a lawyer that specifically did immigration visas for entrepreneurs moving from Australia to the U.S. In the past, UpCounsel wouldn't have been a viable business because a lawyer that specialized couldn't get access to a large enough market within twenty miles of his office. The internet along with tools like blogging, podcasting, and forums has revealed that market.

This is better for consumers, entrepreneurs, *and* lawyers.

Why would you do business with a big advertising agency when you could work with a web marketing agency that intimately understands your industry and business model?

You get all the efficiency improvements, and so do they. The consumer pays less for a better product, and the entrepreneur makes more money.

Jake Puhl runs Firegang Dental Marketing, an agency offering digital marketing services specifically for dentists. Jake previously did digital marketing in a local geographic area (Cincinnati) but decided to work exclusively with dentists.

By working with a single type of *client* instead of a single geographical *area*, he gained a lot of efficiencies that he could pass on in value to the clients both in terms of reduced costs and improved results.

Because he understands the industry, getting clients is easier; they have a smaller group to work with; and word of mouth is more effective. Marketing is easier because other dentists easily identify with existing client case studies.

Fulfilling a job is also done more effectively. Instead of having to go through a period of learning a new client's business every time, they can hit the ground running and start generating results for their clients faster. Dentists all face similar issues in their marketing, so their processes are more streamlined and efficient.

In the past, geography kept these kinds of businesses from

existing, but that's no longer the case. Jake can be based in Seattle and work with clients all over the country.

If you're a dentist, would you meet in person with someone down the street that doesn't understand your business model or industry at all? Or would you rather do a video call with someone on the other side of the country that has an intimate understanding of your business, and knows exactly how to help you get what you're looking for?

While many people would certainly still say the former, more and more are starting to say the latter. The dentist gets a better value, and a business that couldn't have existed a decade ago is now a major opportunity.

Andrew Youderian is the entrepreneur we met in Section 2, who used to be an investment banker. He now runs a business called Right Channel Radios that sells CB Radio equipment. His business model is a 'dropshipping', meaning he sells and markets products from a third party manufacturer. When someone goes to his website and buys, he puts in an order with the manufacturer, who then ships it out to the customer. He's not making the product himself—he created value in his sales, marketing, and customer service processes.

Buying CB radios involves a lot of different factors depending on how you're going to use it. If you don't have a lot of experience with CB Radios, it's hard to know which radio you should order, and as a result he has created educational resources to help people do that.

Google was necessary for his business. If you've got lots of questions about how to buy a radio, you Google them and find Andrew's site. Then you see his helpful articles and figure out which is the right radio for you.

Twenty years ago, there wasn't enough demand in any one geographic area for a CB radio store. If there was, it would have taken a significant amount of capital to set it up. Once he's created the guides for potential customers to read, it costs him pennies to leave them up on his site for anyone to find. If he had to pay a sales or customer service person to explain it repeatedly, his business wouldn't have been profitable. The Long Tail revealed that niche and Andrew took advantage of it.[33]

HOW NEW MARKETS CREATE NEW MARKETS

As the world economy continues to grow, new markets are created then fracture, creating even more new markets. AirBnB was built on the back of Craigslist. Because people would post their rooms for rent on Craigslist, AirBnB would copy over their new listings to Craigslist. People would find out about AirBnB if they were searching for rooms on Craigslist.

They took one section of a bigger marketplace—short term housing on Craigslist—and built a company around it. Just like Jake and Andrew, they were able to serve that "small" market better than Craigslist.

It's not just major tech companies either.

Let's use Eventbrite as an example of a bigger marketplace. Eventbrite is a company that sells event tickets. While they own that particular market, they've opened up whole new markets. You could build a WordPress plugin that does exactly what Eventbrite does, but target it specifically at people in the construction industry that have WordPress sites. That market didn't exist until the last few years when lots of businesses got on Wordpress and became adept at utilizing online services to sell tickets to events.

There are now hundreds of thousands of opportunities like this. These are all opportunities where jobs are going to be replaced by software, and you don't want to be the one with the job—you want to be the one who owns the software.

What's more, these trends are accelerating. There was a 61-year tenure for an average firm in 1958 on the S&P 500; it narrowed to 25 years in 1980—to 18 years now. At the current churn rate, 75% of the S&P 500 will be replaced by 2027.[34] Markets are moving faster. Not only is it easier to enter them because the tools of production are democratizing, but there are also more *to* enter.

The democratization of the tools of production means it's easier to make something. The creation of new markets means there are more and more people to sell those things to, and the democratization of distribution means they are getting easier and easier to reach. Just as jobs are more competitive and threatened than ever, entrepreneurship has become more accessible.

In the next chapter, we'll look at some examples of people that have created businesses built on the back of larger marketplaces and platforms.

CHAPTER 9

THE STAIR STEP METHOD

How to Wade into Entrepreneurship

"Concerning all acts of initiative (and creation), there is one elementary truth, the ignorance of which kills countless ideas and splendid plans: that the moment one definitely commits oneself, then Providence moves too. All sorts of things occur to help one that would never otherwise have occurred. A whole stream of events issues from the decision, raising in one's favor all manner of unforeseen incidents and meetings and material assistance, which no man could have dreamed would have come his way. Whatever you can do, or dream you can do, begin it. Boldness has genius, power, and magic in it. Begin it now."

– WILLIAM HUTCHINSON MURRAY, THE SCOTTISH HIMALAYAN EXPEDITION (1951)

Investing in land, factories, and knowledge was difficult to do early on in their respective eras. Sitting around considering college in the early 1900s, it may not have seemed so hot of an idea. Why get this degree instead of getting a job and making money right away?

Credentialism emerged as the path to invest in knowledge over the course of the twentieth century. It was a social script, a clear path that many of us have followed: go to school, get good grades and extracurriculars, go to college, get a degree, apply for jobs. To someone sitting around in 1900, that wasn't a clear script, but now it is.

The technological and structural changes that have given way to the rise of the Long Tail must be accompanied by social inventions that make it easier to invest in entrepreneurship. As the internet and technology have made entrepreneurship more accessible logistically and technologically, new social scripts are emerging to invest in entrepreneurship just as credentialism and the University system came up a hundred years ago.

The traditional path to acquiring skill sets and relationships is to go to school. You get the credentials; the school connects you with an employer; and then you've got a job. This was always the promise of Ivy League schools: We'll give you the best relationships and the best skillset.

Entrepreneurs are not different. Successful entrepreneurs have great relationships and valuable skillsets. If you have a deep knowledge of Search Engine Optimization and a large network of entrepreneurs who work in that industry, then you won't have any trouble starting a business doing SEO.

But, the entrepreneurial skillset is a bit more nuanced. It falls in the complex square of the Cynefin framework, an emergent practice. You need other skills which still don't have well-defined methods of learning them other than the hard way—actually doing them.

How to manage contractors and employees and their feelings and emotions about the work and your business; how to deal with and overcome the fear around the launch of a new product or making a sales call; how to psychologically manage cash flow issues.

You also need a different type of relationship: relationships with other entrepreneurs. Having relationships in your industry is important, but it's equally important to have relationships with other people working in the same framework that you are. They let you see new business models, uncover new opportunities, and support you as you support them.

In short, you need an entrepreneurial network and an entrepreneurial track record.

There are, in reality, hundreds of ways to acquire an entrepreneurial network and skillset. I won't pretend this is a comprehensive guide.

But as entrepreneurship becomes more popular, there are

more examples and scripts to follow. Two have emerged as the most prominent: The Stair Step Method and Apprenticeships.

THE STAIR STEP METHOD

In the past, starting a business required a big upfront investment—both in terms of time and money. Entrepreneurship was an all or nothing affair. Humans, risk-averse creatures that we are, always found that a tough proposition.

The technology that's facilitated the Long Tail has made it possible to wade your way into entrepreneurship now as opposed to jumping in headfirst. The decreasing technological hurdles to jump over, like lower startup costs and more niche opportunities, mean starting a business is easier than it's ever been.

Many full-blown entrepreneurs today started freelancing on the side, then transitioned to consulting or freelancing full time, and some have chosen to release their own products.

Rob Walling, who now runs three software companies and hosts Startups for The Rest of Us, a podcast for other software-minded entrepreneurs, created the Stair Step framework to explain his path into entrepreneurship and has found it's applied broadly to other entrepreneurs he's seen.

The first step in the Stair Step Method, as Rob explains it, is launching a product that sells for a one-time fee and has a single marketing channel: SEO (search engine optimization), paid advertising like Google Adwords or Facebook ads, a blog audience, or **Amazon.com**.

Once you've gotten experience building and launching one product in a small, less competitive environment where you've built your confidence, you can start to expand your toolbelt of relationships and skills.

You've got a product and it's making money.

Step two is launching enough of those one-time products that you're able to buy your time back. You can either quit consulting if you're a consultant, or quit your job if you're employed. At that point you've got confidence in building and marketing a business. You've gotten through the fear that comes with a launch. You have a virtual assistant you hired on UpWork helping you with customer support, and you've learned to manage them.

More importantly, you have a lot of time. Now you're at step three. Instead of working nights and weekends like you had been, you've got 40–60 hours a week to put in on your business, giving you a platform to launch bigger products, and projects from. That could be a SaaS business, bigger eCommerce business, or a membership site.

Rob got started as an entrepreneur by quitting his corporate job and moving into consulting as a computer programmer. As a consultant, he learned how to better sell himself, manage his time, and understand the basics of running a business.

Then around 2000, Rob started launching products but without a lot of success. In 2005 he acquired some invoicing software that was in an alpha version, full of bugs and making a few hundred dollars a month from a handful of not-very-happy customers.

He didn't know how to market it, but he saw the original owners had done some SEO and he started to build on that. Using SEO alone, he was able to get the business generating two to four thousand dollars a month.

At that point he had some experience in SEO and talking with customers. It also gave him some capital to work with, as well as some much-needed confidence in launching and marketing products. With that experience, he knew that he had SEO and a bit of Adwords knowledge in his tool belt.

Because he had more money than time (since he was still consulting), he started scouting for other businesses to buy. He bought an eCommerce website selling bath towels that he grew from zero to $2500 a month in profit. He bought a business creating website themes that he built up to $2500 in profit. He had a niche job board for electricians that he built up using SEO and another app that built wedding websites.

In each case, he was adding tools to his tool belt: hiring and managing contractors, dealing with customers, buying banner ads and Facebook ads, SEO, and Google Adwords. He was also building his confidence as an entrepreneur, learning how to deal with customers and launch products.

He parlayed that into a personal brand with his blog, **SoftwareByRob.com**, and podcast, Startups for the Rest of Us.[35] Both have helped him connect with thousands of other entrepreneurs—some of whom are now customers of one or more of his software products.

From there he bought a struggling SEO tool, HitTail, and revitalized it using everything he'd learned in earlier businesses to grow it by 1000% over the course of the next year. He used Facebook ads, partnerships, banner ads, and SEO—all skills he'd acquired running his smaller businesses.

Now he's building Drip, a larger SaaS app than HitTail, that does email marketing automation.

Over the course of his career, he stair stepped his way up into bigger and better businesses.

That ability to stair step has never been possible before. It's only become possible in the last ten years due to the effects of the democratization of distribution and production, along with the creation of new markets.

Before the internet, you would have had to buy a physical location, hire staff, and the pressure was on. You better make it work, and fast: it was going to consume all your time and a lot of capital. If it failed, you had invested tens of thousands of dollars and probably a couple of years of time. Now you can dip your toes in the water and gradually wade into entrepreneurship. You can start investing nights and weekends working on step one products. A few of these successful products got Rob to full-time on his business, even with a mortgage and a family to support.[36]

Rob had a moment of realization when he kept trying to build his first purchase, the invoicing software, into a ten-thousand-dollars-per-month business. It stalled out, oscillating between two and four thousand dollars a month. After spending 18 months trying to grow it, he realized that he had tapped out the market.

Part of what the internet has done is release a lot of latent demand that was never economically viable to fulfill in the past. The invoicing software is for a very niche market. When you were dealing with a lot of fixed startup costs, like a lease on a building or buying servers, it simply wasn't a viable business.

Ramit Sethi, a financial blogger turned business consultant, launched a course teaching people in jobs how to earn an extra $1,000 per month freelancing around their day jobs.

Ramit found that if he could get people to earn $1,000 on the side, then many of them would gain the confidence and resources to "stair step" their way further into entrepreneurship.

Once they get $1,000 month, it felt possible to double it to $2,000 per month, and once their side income replaces their corporate income, most of them choose to leave their jobs.

Because of services like cloud computing, SaaS and contractors make it much easier to keep expenses down. Millions of niches like invoicing software are now viable step one businesses, where you can build up a skillset and cash flow with very little competition to launch into bigger opportunities.

It also means that you have to stair step up. The market targeted by the invoicing software simply wasn't big enough to support a ten thousand dollar a month business.

The most important takeaways, however, are the principles of the method. Start with a relatively ambitious but discrete opportunity, and use that to build out your skillset and relationships for the next project.

Rob specializes in helping technical entrepreneurs stair step their way out of consulting or their jobs by building WordPress plugins, and he's seen a lot of them become successful.

Richard Chen built **phpgrid.com**, a grid control that links in really well with the web programming language PHP, and was able to leverage it so he could earn enough to move his family from LA to Singapore.

Now you may be asking, what the heck is a "grid control that links in really well with PHP?"

Exactly. It's a hyper niche product that couldn't have existed five or ten years ago.

David Hehenberger founded FatCat Apps using two Wordpress plugins, Easy Pricing Tables and Easy Opt-Ins, which let him employ a full-time developer in Vietnam and focus on growing his business instead of consulting.

For technical founders, plugins (specifically those on WordPress) are the most common way to stair step their ways out.

There are other examples outside of just software and plugins.

Andrew Youderian who runs Right Channel Radios, stair stepped his way up in eCommerce.

He expanded that expertise and those relationships into starting a similar dropshipping business selling trolling motors, and now runs **eCommerceFuel.com** where he helps other eCommerce Entreprenurs grow their eCommerce businesses.[37]

Nathan Barry, a designer and author, stair stepped his way from his job as a designer into running his own business by writing two books on design, *The App Design Handbook* and *Designing Web Applications*.

After he saw that many people were interested in his strategy for publishing high priced eBooks (the book started at $39), he wrote another book on that, *Authority*, his most successful ever. Now he is growing ConvertKit, a software product designed to help authors with email marketing.[38]

John McIntyre was working as an intern at a resort in the Philippines when someone asked him to write an email autoresponder, a series of five emails designed to help new prospects convert into customers. After the first one was successful, he started marketing the service and launched a productized service[39] selling email marketing and conversion consulting to business owners.[40]

Dan Norris also launched a productized service similar to John with WP Curve, though targeted at a much larger audience and from a lower price point.

While all the business models are unique, what's universal is that the barrier to entry in each is no longer capital or formal credentials. All they needed to get started were free or relatively cheap resources they could buy online, and their own hard work.

The entrepreneurial leap has become the entrepreneurial stair step. The latent demand and lower barriers to entry have allowed more people to become entrepreneurs by easing their way into the process. That's not to say it's easy—you still have to climb the stairs, but no longer in a single bound.

Stair Stepping lets you build momentum behind your trajectory by developing the skills you need to run an entrepreneurial company. It also lets you develop relationships. While it's difficult to meet other likeminded individuals first starting out, once you begin to create a track record of results, people become curious about those results and want to work with you, learn from you, or just hang out and talk about how you've done what you've done.

CHAPTER 10

THE RETURN OF APPRENTICESHIPS

THE OTHER SOCIAL SCRIPT THAT IS EMERGING (OR rather re-emerging) is apprenticeships. For thousands of years leading up to 1900, careers were started not by degrees, but in apprenticing. Benjamin Franklin started his career as an apprentice in his older brother's print shop. He stair stepped his way into owning his own print shop before moving into politics and foreign affairs.[41]

In Medieval Europe, it was traditional for aspiring tradesman to apply for apprenticeships with a master of their craft. They would go to work in the master's shop, usually for around seven years, before passing into the journeyman phase where they were required to do a project that they would submit for review to their prospective guild. If they passed, they'd be accepted as a master who could start the whole cycle over by taking apprentices. This was the way skill sets were passed on among families and communities.

In that sense, apprenticing today works on the same premise as stair stepping—it's a way to build skillsets and relationships. While stair stepping works on the premise of having some alternative source of income—be it consulting/freelancing or a job—and investing that in building products, apprenticing is based on the idea of aligning your primary source of income with building skillsets and relationships.

The premise is pretty straight forward: you find someone that is doing what you would like to be doing in five to ten years and cut them a deal: "I'll come work for you for relatively cheap and I'll create results you would normally have to pay a lot more for, in exchange I get to train at altitude. I get to see the inside of how your business works: how you launch products, what the industry looks like, and who I need to know." Instead of playing with your own money (like what you would need from consulting, a job, or savings), you play with house money.

Apprenticing was how I got started in entrepreneurship. I taught myself a bit of Search Engine Optimization using Moz's Beginner's Guide to SEO, a free guide online. I paid $20 to get a hosting account from **GoDaddy.com** and built a website outside my job at the time, as an English teacher. I cold-emailed a handful of marketing agencies and used those sites as proof of my skills. That turned into a part-time internship, and eventually a full-time job where I learned a lot about internet marketing, project management, and technology.

I went and worked in another small entrepreneurial company

for two years, where I got to move from SEO to Marketing Manager to running a small division.

I was able to acquire entrepreneurial skills by being on the inside of an entrepreneurial company.

Unbeknownst to me until very late in the game, it turned out I was investing into entrepreneurship.

Charlie Hoehn originally worked with business coach Ramit Sethi and then author Tim Ferriss as an apprentice for a few years before publishing a book, *Play It Away.*

The New York Times bestselling author Ryan Holiday apprenticed for Robert Greene, author of five international bestsellers including *The 48 Laws of Power* and *Seduction*, before launching his own best selling book, *Trust Me, I'm Lying*.

I've seen dozens of other entrepreneurs come up through an apprenticeship in much the same way.

ADVANTAGES OF APPRENTICESHIPS TO THE APPRENTICE

1. Relationships.

One common mistake early entrepreneurs make is that they think they need a business idea. That's rarely the case: you don't need a business idea—you need *relationships*. As you acquire relationships and entrepreneurial experience, ideas will become a bigger problem, but not in the way you think.

Experienced entrepreneurs frequently deal with "shiny object syndrome," a phenomenon where they see too many opportunities and have too many ideas, and not enough resources to pursue them.

I've never met someone that has a lot of strong entrepreneurial relationships that was hurting for ideas. Samuel Hulick got started by working with Rob Walling when Rob was launching Drip. By doing a brief apprenticeship, he realized that user onboarding for SaaS apps was a major pain point, so he launched **UserOnboard.com** to help SaaS companies with their onboarding process.

2. More Effective in Complex Environments

While credentialism was an effective system for teaching people to operate effectively in the complicated domain—one where good practices can be measured and cause and effect can be correlated—it hasn't proved an effective system for teaching people to operate in the complex domain.

When I first began working for other entrepreneurs, I was shocked when they would commit tens or hundreds of thousands dollars towards "gut" feelings. The nature of complex systems is that often the best ideas and approaches aren't ones that can be taught, but are the result of experience in the domain. In his book *Ready, Fire, Aim*, Michael Masterson advises companies to develop new products by having the CEO sit down and brainstorm the top possible ideas based on their intuition. It's usually by interacting with the market for ten years that great new products come about. No one can teach that, but an apprenticeship lets you stare, and fiddle, with the market on someone else's dime.

3. Better Value AKA Play with House Money

Instead of paying six figures to go to law school or get an MBA, you can get paid to learn skills and build relationships valued by the marketplace.

Apprenticeships are also an astoundingly good value right now.

Many people think free work or unpaid internships are exploitative, but find the idea of someone taking out a quarter million in debt to get a college degree and an MBA a smart investment.

That may be a legacy of the knowledge economy that we haven't adapted to yet.

ADVANTAGES OF APPRENTICESHIPS TO ENTREPRENEURIAL COMPANIES

It's certainly important to have tight hiring practices, as many applicants fall into the camp of people who like the idea of being an entrepreneur, but may not be willing to make the sacrifices. There's a large number of people who are willing to make the sacrifices and do the work at an exceptional value.

1. Less risk for employers.

A large part of the employment model as it exists today is

built on a traditional model where companies expect to hire someone and retain them for the majority of their career. As a result they end up investing heavily in new hire for the first few years, expecting the investment to pay off in the long run.

What frequently happens instead is that employees come into a company, get the benefit of being trained, and then leave the company for another opportunity. Companies react by getting upset and respond by working on better retention programs.

Instead of companies getting upset because people leave, why not rework the equation to plan on people being there for two to five years instead of twenty to fifty? Instead of trying to swim upstream with better retention programs, companies can adapt by creating apprenticeship programs.

Agreements can be structured around the basis of having people come in for pre-structured timelines. If you know someone is only going to be there two to five years, you can negotiate a contract where both parties win on that basis, usually by paying less money up front but giving them access to industry knowledge and relationships.

2. You attract higher quality applicants.

If you measure the output of a sales team of ten people, it will inevitably fall close to the 80/20 rule.

Two of the ten will generate around eighty percent of the sales. While the difference in impact is most obvious in a role where numbers can be closely tracked—such as sales—apprenticeships are built on the idea that if you can bring more of the most talented individuals into an organization, albeit for a shorter time, the output will make it more than worth it.

Apprenticeships enable entrepreneurial companies to bring in young, talented, hungry individuals to make a trade. The young entrepreneur agrees to give their best energy in growing the company for a few years and sees it as an investment in their entrepreneurial future. The employer is able to bring someone into the company that isn't looking for a traditional job, but is happy to invest in themselves through working for someone else that will help them reach their potential exchange by building relationships and a skillset at a value employers couldn't get in the general labor market.

3. You build an alumni network of smart, ambitious people.

Another advantage that companies have seen is the creation of alumni networks and networked intelligence. Ambitious former apprentices go on to build their own companies or work with other entrepreneurs, gradually creating more relationships to tap into.

We've seen this model before in coaching trees. Great sports coaches like Bill Belichick of the New England Patriots have long used the apprenticeship model. They make an offer to young coaches: instead of taking a second-tier head coaching job, come take a top-tier assistant coaching job for two to five years. The young coaches have an opportunity to study and experience a championship system and build relationships with the other coaches. The experienced coach is able to bring the most talented young coaches to inject new innovation into their systems and slowly build a network. If you look at the current head coaches in the NBA or NFL, the 80/20 rule applies. 80% of them usually have common roots in apprenticing with 20% of the head coaches of the past generation.

Technology startups have started to develop "mafias," or groups of successful entrepreneurs that can trace their roots back to a common source. Elon Musk (Currently of SpaceX and Tesla), Reid Hoffman (LinkedIn), and Peter Thiel (Palantir) all worked together at PayPal.[42]

TRAJECTORY THEORY—A GUIDE TO HIRING AN APPRENTICE (OR GETTING HIRED)

Three-time *The New York Times* bestselling author Tucker Max has hired a lot of people to work in an apprentice-type position, and they've almost always gone on to be successful in future projects and companies. Why is his track record so good?

In his words, he hires "people who have done things."

I apprenticed at one company that I had already interviewed with for a job nine months earlier. After the first go around, they told me, "You're pretty smart, but you don't really have any applicable skills."

So I started building websites about home furnishings and

selling advertising space using Google's Adsense program on them. That led to working with a local marketing agency.

When I re-applied for the apprenticeship, I had built a few websites and used that experience to get a job at a marketing agency, where I became a project manager.

They saw that as trajectory and hired me.

Charlie Hoehn did much the same thing. When he applied to work with Tim Ferriss, he was working with Ramit Sethi and was able to show that work to Ferriss.

THE APPRENTICESHIP HIRING PROCESS

Here's an example of a process I've used before to hire for an apprenticeship position. It should give both sides an idea of what to expect.

Define Standard Operating Procedures that the Apprentice Will Take Over

- You want someone to be able to come in and have set processes and documentation in order to put them at full-time (~40 hours) right off the bat executing on processes with defined ROI

- Create a spreadsheet with three columns for the executive team to make sure the position is clearly defined.

→ Column 1—The process to be taken over (Ex. Adwords management, Send Email Newsletter, customer support requests, etc.)

→ Column 2—The estimated time for the task each week

→ Column 3—An estimate of what it's worth to the company (Defined SOPs should all be defined cash flows with positive ROI to ensure that the position is profitable as soon as possible.)

→ *Note:* Each task should have documentation built out for it in a pre-defined SOP

Executive Team Discusses Job Description and SOPs

- Do we have cash flow to pay for the person for two years including raises, etc.?
- Is this a Heck Yes? Even a high quality hire usually takes three to six months to get up to speed, so it has to be a Heck Yes decision.
- How confident are we? Can we prove that defined SOPs are positive ROI cash flows?

Write a Job Description

- Write it like a sales letter selling the benefits of the position.

Far too many companies spend massive resources marketing their products, but none marketing their opportunities.

- Examples of Good Hiring Pages for Apprenticeships
    - → http://www.tropicalmba.com/work-with-us/
    - → http://wpcurve.com/content-marketing-job/
    - → http://www.appsumo.com/hireme/
    - → http://benhebert.com/success-champion/
    - → http://bookinabox.com/hire-me
    - → http://empireflippers.com/marketplace-apprentice-wanted/

Post Job Description/Sales Letter

- **Important Note:** Don't oversell the mentorship aspect or you'll wind up with applicants looking for a lot of your time; the value of the position is "training at altitude"—getting to work on bigger projects than if they were using their own money.

- Application Requirements: Use a centralized form; Google Forms work fine, but you can use Typeform or Gravity Forms as well. The important thing is to get all the applications in one space. Require the following fields:

- Name
- Email
- A two-minute Youtube video—Youtube videos let you get a much better feel for someone than reading a stale application, and many people can be disqualified after employers watch the first five to ten seconds and ask if the applicant was someone they would ever be willing to have lunch with.
    - Ask them to say why they want the job, why they think they would be a good fit; also ask them to explain any previous projects they've worked on that offer relevant experience.
    - This can be posted on Youtube as "unlisted," and a URL entered into the form.
- Any position specific questions
    - Include an Instant Disqualifier: Ask applicants to include the word "cafe" in response to one of these.
        - Example: "Include the word Cafe as the first word in response to question 5—What's your experience with Wordpress?"
- Link to blog/social media accounts/anything else they want to share

    - Make sure they set the accounts to "Open" or equivalent so you can actually look at them.

  - → Skype ID

  - → Earliest Possible Start Date

  - → Links to Examples of Previous Work; this can be anything they've done before (you're looking for trajectory)

Promote the Job Description

- Post a copy of the job description on relevant job boards and drive them back to the primary form.

  - → Craigslist—Though frequently maligned, Craigslist often has some of the highest quality applicants

  - → EscapetheCity.org—Hiring platform for corporate types looking to leave traditional corporate jobs, primarily UK.

  - → Your Personal Blog (if applicable)

  - → Your Company Blog (if applicable)

  - → Relevant Industry Forums

- Promote it through your personal network—I've seen the majority of successful apprentices come through friends of friends, so promote it on Facebook and Twitter. People that are friends or friends of friends are more likely to be a good value match for the company.

Allow Two to Three Weeks for Applications and Actively Market the Position

While it's live, actively market the position to get as many applicants as possible. Effective filtering will let you get down to the most qualified candidates later so the more applicants, the better.

Application Evaluation

- Filter out using the Instant Disqualifier.
    - → Usually 80–90% of applicants won't include the instant disqualifier (starting a response with a certain word) in their application. Inability to follow basic instructions is a great way to weed out people and includes a tragically large amount of the general population.
- Watch the Youtube Videos
    - → Go through the applicant's' videos and look through supplemental materials.
        - Gut Check/Gut Sense—What's your thin slicing/

gut impression? Delete everyone that you wouldn't want to go to lunch with.

- Criteria for evaluation—Set-up a spreadsheet and grade each of the following on a scale of 1–10
    - You want someone that's focused on business and long-term growth—not just getting out of a job they don't like.
    - What have they done? Best predictor of future success is past success.
    - Heck yes or no—Do they have the potential to be best-in-class at their position in three to five years?
    - Do they match up with the company's core values?
    - Must have a positive outlook—moving towards motivated, not away from it. Warning signs are talking bad about their current condition and how they are trying to get away from it.
- Get your list down to the top four to twelve candidates for interviews depending on how many applicants you have. There is typically a clear top tier of applicants that are worth interviewing, and it usually constitutes 3–7% of the total applicant pool.

Set up Interviews with Top Candidates

- Schedule aggressively; don't let the hiring process drag on if it can be avoided.
- Send a link to all applicants you want to interview and request that they choose from the available time slots. Tools like Meetme.so and Calendly will let you set up available times for them to schedule.
    - → If none of those time slots work, ask them to propose times that will work for them.

Interview

- Preparation and Guidelines
    - → Re-Watch their video once more and jot down any specific questions for them
    - → Request a video interview rather than audio; a lot is communicated via body language and nonverbal cues
    - → If you smell fish in the application, go after it
    - → Dig into past experience; past success is the greatest predictor of future success
    - → Start with three to five minutes of small talk to get them comfortable

- Primary Questions
    - → Why do you want this job? What's most valuable and exciting to you about this opportunity?
        - ▪ Evaluating for: Long-term focus? Business focus? What do you know about our company? Are our values the same?
    - → What motivates you? What gets you out of bed in the morning?
        - ▪ Evaluating for: You want to figure out their "WHY." Watch out for folks who are running away from their problems; look for people pursuing opportunities.
    - → Where do you see yourself in five years? What are your long-term goals and objectives?
        - ▪ Look for high trajectory, ambitious individuals.
    - → What experience do you have relevant to this position?
        - ▪ Evaluating for: A better feel for their industry expertise
    - → What's the most difficult thing you think you've ever accomplished? What are you most proud of?
        - ▪ Evaluating for: How they actually interacted in a

real-world situation and what they consider difficult. Again, "people that have done stuff."

- → What have some of the biggest influences on your life been—could be books, people, events, anything.
  - ▪ Evaluating for: Inflection points
    - ◊ Are they on a steep trajectory or are they doing roughly the same stuff now that they were five years ago?
- → Do you have any questions for me? Any questions about the position?
  - ▪ Evaluating for: They should take an interest and show they've actually thought about the position and how it matches up with their skillset and trajectory.

- Special Circumstances Questions
  - → For the people that are farther along: Why do they want this job?
    - ▪ Are you committed to staying for at least a couple of years?
    - ▪ Do you know it doesn't pay a lot?

        - If they've been in the game a long time and haven't made anything happen, figure out why.

    - → Ask any additional questions based specifically on their application

- Record Notes/Thoughts

    - → At the end of the interview, write down notes and thoughts on the candidate.

- Re-grade them on a scale of one to five on the following five criteria:

    - → Past Work—What have they done?

        - Doesn't necessarily need to be domain specific; look for motivation and work ethic.

        - Again, the best predictor of future success is past success

    - → Trajectory Personal and Business—Where are they going? Does it align with where the company and position are going?

    - → Value Match—Do their core values align with ours? (Most important)

    - → Domain Experience—Do they have relevant domain experience? (Least important)

→ Gut Check/Gut Sense—What's your thin slicing/ gut impression?

Note: If you're interested in an apprenticeship, grade yourself on these five criteria. Do you have a history of work you've accomplished to show? Are you on a trajectory that would make you attractive to hire as an apprentice?

Interview Evaluation

- Put together a list of three finalists to discuss with relevant people in the executive management team or with a trusted friend if possible.

- Everyone talks over the candidates

  → Clarify upsides/downsides

- If there's no clear leader, schedule a follow-up call to dig into any potential liabilities or clarify outstanding questions.

  → If you smell fish, go after it hard this time. Dig into anything that could be problematic.

  → You want to play devil's advocate at this point—this job is going to be hard, the pay sucks, you have to be here for two years, etc.

    - Even after all this, they should still be super excited.[43]

IN SUMMARY (A.K.A TL;DR)

The short story of technology and the Long Tail is this: Fifty years ago, you needed major media like NBC to produce videos and distribute it to millions of people. Now it doesn't. The same is true of almost every class of media and product.

1. It's cheaper to make something.

2. It's easier and cheaper than ever to reach those markets.

3. There are new markets willing to buy those things.

What's scarce isn't capital. It takes a lot of capital to start a factory in China. The expensive infrastructure is all sitting in server farms in Silicon Valley or in a factory in China. The important value to be added is through creativity and entrepreneurship.

All the profit margins in business increasingly go to the individuals doing the innovative, creative, entrepreneurial work. Entrepreneurship is becoming more accessible just as jobs are becoming more competitive. Even as more corporations shed full time positions to hire temps or contractors, there are more businesses, and they're doing better with every passing year. These significant trends are also all accelerating. At some point, the two will intersect.

The scarce resource—entrepreneurship—can be invested in more easily than ever.

You are now sitting at a nexus where your cost basis is very low, but your profits are very high if you're an entrepreneur. Let's look more closely at what those profits look like.

SECTION V

Entrepreneurship Is More Profitable than Ever

The Future of Work

"I don't think of work as work or play as play. It's all just living."

– RICHARD BRANSON

A BRIEF HISTORY OF WORK AND JOBS

If we look at modern day pre-neolithic, hunter/gatherer groups, they don't "have jobs" or "do work" in the sense we think about them today. They did what they have to do to survive and different members have different roles. These roles aren't seen as a disutility, something to actively be avoided that should be balanced by utilities, or things we want to do. They are merely a part of life, they're integral, integrated into the broader life experience.

In most cases, they hunted and gathered as needed. They spent a lot of time socializing and playing when there is already enough food to be had for the next few days.

The idea of jobs as we understand them today is a product of two major inflection points in human history.

The first is the beginning of recorded history itself: the Neolithic Revolution, when humans transitioned from nomadic hunter/gatherers to settled farming communities.

A nomadic hunter/gatherer does just enough work to survive. Once he has enough food for the day or week, he's apt to go spend time socializing or playing. Constantly on the move and unable to store food, anything he accumulates more than a few days in advance will rot.

This conception of work and jobs is one that is still embraced by many individuals in developing nations. During a visit to the Mekong Delta in Southern Vietnam, I was informed by a woman living there that it was common for men to go to work for the first few days of the week and, once they knew they had enough money to survive the rest of the week, to stop showing up and stay home with their families or, more likely, drink beer with their friends.

Once we moved into settled farming communities, work took on a different dynamic. A peasant tilling the fields worked in a way that a hunter/gatherer wouldn't understand. Work for a serf or peasant never ends. Once we moved from a nomadic to settled existence, we began to accumulate wealth. If a farmer can store grain, he works more, so he can accumulate more wealth.

More wealth leads to larger families, which needed to be fed. A cycle of increasing family size and community requiring more material wealth began. This ability to accumulate and store wealth resulted in a fundamental shift to work and jobs. Even though tilling the fields may not have been desirable, it did allow an individual to start accumulating wealth and power in a way that a hunter/gatherer couldn't.

It wasn't a decision that Neolithic cultures consciously made because they were happier or more fulfilled. It was one that led to economic prosperity and power. The societies that encouraged that behavior won out by force.[44]

With the rise of Neolithic societies, work came to be seen as a curse, something to be avoided. In one of the oldest existing books, the Bible, after the fall of the Garden of Eden Genesis 3:19 laments that: "By the sweat of your brow you will eat your food until you return to the ground."

The Greeks also saw work as a curse. The Greek god of hard labor was *Ponos*, taken from the Latin *poena* for sorrow. Manual labor was for slaves, and hard work was looked down upon. Plato and Aristotle believed work was for the majority so that the elite might "engage in pure exercises of the mind—art, philosophy, and politics."

This change was accelerated with the Industrialization of society.

Work became more and more like jobs as we understand them now. It was a natural side effect of the advancement of civilization. As the demand for specialized labor arose with the Industrial Revolution, individuals began doing more and more specific tasks.

The Industrial Revolution and the factory dramatically increased the amount of wealth someone could accumulate by making the creation of goods much more efficient, and thus cheaper to the consumer. As the Neolithic Revolution let individuals start saving material wealth, the Industrial Revolution accelerated this trend.

Like the hunter/gatherers that moved to settled communities, they weren't choosing the new forms of work out of a search for self-actualization—they were choosing it because it effectively addressed the economic limit in their society and it gave them a better quality of life. An English factory worker in 1900 was materially better off than his farming ancestors two hundred years earlier. He had access to more consumer goods, more cheaply than his grandfather could have imagined.

Your great grandparents, were they alive, would find it hard to wrap their minds around the levels of choice and convenience we have today.

DECOUPLING INPUT FROM OUTPUT

Henry Ford discovered by giving his workers a raise to $5 an hour, Ford was able to dramatically reduce turnover and increase output at his factories.[45]

For most of the 20th century, this trend continued. Workers in jobs continued to earn more and produce more. The promise of the Industrial Revolution was being fulfilled.

People chose to engage in this work because it made them wealthier. A factory worker earning $5 per hour in Ford's factory had a wealthier life than his grandfather, the sharecropper. He could provide for his family whether the crops were bad or good.

Yet, over the past two hundred years, work hours in the West have been slowly, but steadily decreasing.

According to the U.S. Department of the Interior and research done on census reports, the average work week in 1830 was almost seventy hours, gradually falling to sixty hours by the turn of the 20th century. It continued to fall until reaching around forty hours per week in 1940. It's since remained there.[46]

As technology has improved, an increase in sheer quantity of hours failed to generate more wealth creation or greater productivity.

The work needed to address the new limit, and entrepreneurial work is qualitatively different. It's different in kind, not degree.

The traditional job-based, simple and complicated work of "do X get Y" model has ceased being effective.

THE TOM SAWYER EFFECT

In Mark Twain's *The Adventures of Huckleberry Finn,* Tom Sawyer is confronted with the prospect of being forced to paint his Aunt Polly's fence.

Carefully repositioning his explanation of the work to his friends, Tom is able to convince them to pay him to paint the fence and then collect from Aunt Polly. "It'll be fun!" he insists.

Effectively, Sawyer turned the task from an obligation for himself to a choice for his friends.

Economists have come to call this the Tom Sawyer Effect.

It illustrates a simple lesson: As humans, we love to work but dislike the obligation of it—the job-based paradigm.

For roughly the past three thousand years that paradigm has been one that has addressed the economic limit and increased material well-being, so we've accepted it.

Because it led to a better overall quality of life, we've accepted work as a disutility because it was necessary to survive as a society and a worthy trade off for us as individuals.

Working in a factory or corporation in a major city was something many individuals aspired to during the early 20th century for the economic prosperity relative to a more tenuous farming life.

Yet, as we've seen, the limit has shifted. Economic growth has stalled both for society and for us as individuals. Because of the qualitative and structural changes to the economy, it's getting harder to find jobs, they're more risky, and they're less profitable.

In the past, we have accepted the disutility of jobs and sought balanced living because it's addressed the limit. It's allowed us to accumulate more wealth.

What has changed is that the kind of work needed to advance society taps into fundamental human drives now. Complex, entrepreneurial work is both more valuable and more in line with traditional human drives.

Suppressing fundamental human motivators was a three-thousand-year-old anomaly that's now coming to a close.

MORE MONEY, MORE FREEDOM, AND MORE MEANING

As history shows, we are fundamentally driven to acquire more material wealth, since the agricultural era. Having all the material goods we need is important.

However, that's not the only thing that's important to us.

When we look at the collected research for fundamental human motivations over the past few decades, as well as historical examples, it generally comes down to three core motivators: money, freedom, and meaning.

Money is really just a proxy for general material wealth, but it's a pretty accurate proxy and medium of exchange. However, once we reach a certain level of material abundance, popularly cited at about $75,000 per year in personal income, it becomes dramatically less motivating to us and there are two core drivers that people tap into: meaning and freedom.[47]

Many of the richest individuals in history retire into

philanthropy searching for more meaning in helping others and freedom for themselves in the process.

John Rockefeller, Andrew Carnegie, Warren Buffett, and Bill Gates were more interested in philanthropy and freedom to spend time with their families and pursue hobbies than making more money after they'd amassed a Scrooge-Mc-Duck-worthy pool of money.

Because of the structural economic changes discussed earlier, meaning and freedom aren't just luxuries to be put off later in life after you've "put in your time."

Instead, they're potentialities to be harnessed. If we can structure meaning and freedom into our work now, we see the Tom Sawyer Effect—work goes from being an obligation to a choice. It's no longer something we're obligated to do, but something we seek out. It's a utility to integrate into our lives instead of a disutility to be balanced. As a result, the quality of the work is better. Freedom and meaning aren't something to be put off until after you're rich—they help you get rich.

By harnessing freedom and meaning earlier in our careers and putting it into our work, we can now live freer, more meaningful lives that help others, and get rich doing it.

CHAPTER 11

MORE MONEY

The Economics of Entrepreneurship

A BRITISH ECONOMIST RELEASED A STUDY BASED ON THE past 2000 years of human economic history. In the study, he examined trends illuminating an inevitable conclusion: the human species is doomed to starvation. We've reached the carrying capacity of the planet.

As the planet's population continues to expand, we'll be faced with an inability to produce enough food. Mass starvation will eventually bring the population back to sustainable levels, which is not comforting to those who don't make the cut.

His conclusion is based on undisputed historical data, verified by sources across the globe.

The British economist was Thomas Malthus and the study

was the *Essay on Principle of Population*, which he penned two hundred years ago in 1798.

Malthus believed population growth was such a powerful force that eventually it would outpace man's ability to keep up, resulting in a return to subsistence level conditions. More and more people would be born into a world that couldn't possibly keep up with feeding them.

So far, Malthus's prediction hasn't panned out.

In the two hundred years since Malthus made his prediction, not only has man's ability to produce kept up with population growth—it's been outpaced by a factor of thirty times or more.

The global population has increased by over six billion while, at the same time, each individual has more wealth than their grandparents could have ever imagined. GDP per capita, a measure of wealth at an individual level, has gone from around $300 a year to over $6000 a year globally, and over $25,000 a year in the U.S. and the rest of the West over the course of the past two hundred years.

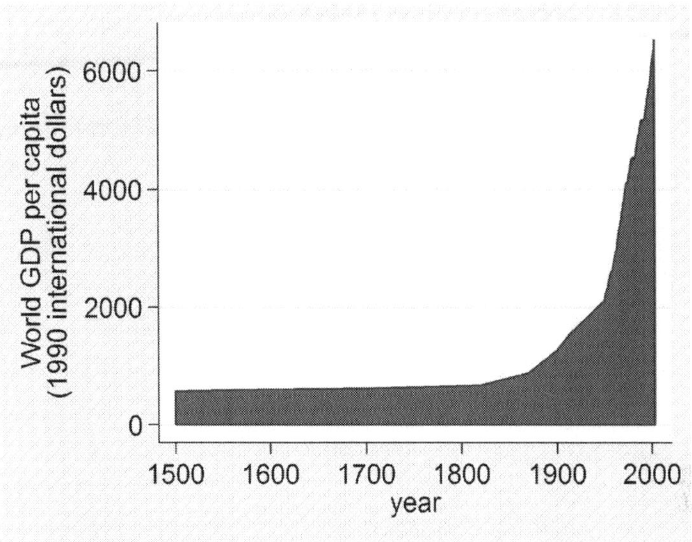

https://en.wikipedia.org/wiki/Poverty_reduction#/media/File:World_GDP_per_capita_1500_to_2003.png

The tangible result is the level of material wealth that we all have at our fingertips today. Our grandparents couldn't even imagine consumer goods and service like smartphones or two-day delivery from Amazon, things we now largely take for granted.

And yet we still haven't incorporated Malthus's error into our world view.

My family rarely, if ever, talked about money when I was growing up.

Talking about money is still taboo in many households, a necessary evil.

This isn't without historical precedent.

Usury—money lending—was considered a sin in the Catholic Church for most of its existence. Since Catholics in Europe were forbidden from lending money, many Jews, such as the Rothschilds, became bankers.

Any society where money (as a proxy for wealth) is a limited resource would do well to prevent people from loaning it to one another. If wealth is limited, which it was for most of human history until around 1800, then a loan can only result in one party losing and the other winning.

If I loan you money and there's a limited supply of it, you can only pay me back by taking that money from someone else, who must then take it from someone else, and on we go in a downward spiral.

Our understanding of money and wealth creation as a society is rooted in pre-industrial notions. Charities ask businesses and community members to "give back," implying that they took something to begin with. This belief doesn't conform very well to the way money and wealth behaves in the modern world.

With the Industrial Revolution, humanity invented wealth creation. That is, we invented the ability to make more wealth. With plenty of bumps along the way, the world's GDP per capita has been compounding at around 1–2% for a couple hundred years. On average, everyone has been getting wealthier for the past two centuries.

This doesn't seem like a large number, but it's led to the explosion in wealth we've seen over the course of the 20th century and the quality of consumer life we have today compared to a European serf three centuries ago.

Technology, namely computers and the internet, have yet again compounded this ability. It's now easier to create wealth and value, a somewhat new-agey way to say "get rich and make money," than at any time in history.

All the factors covered in the previous chapters mean that starting a business that can return 20%, 30%, or 100% annually with low upfront costs, though not easy, isn't a far-fetched dream like it might have been fifty years ago.

Yet our behavior and thinking about how money works, and how to get rich, are still based on an antiquated worldview.

THE BAKER VS. FIXED PIE MINDSET

Imagine you've been stranded on a deserted island with a fishing pole. You have drinking water, but no food. At rest, your body uses energy equivalent to one fish per day to survive. You have to work to catch fish, but each day you fish, you need an additional fish to compensate for the energy used up. If you catch two fish per day, you will live. If you catch less, you die.

If you catch a third fish, you can rest the next day or you can start to store up fish so you can take a day off and make a net to improve your productivity. The extra fish, the profit, gives you the option to do something else.

Profit, then, is simply the difference between the consumption and production of a living thing—be it human, business, or animal. All living things must be profitable.

We survive unprofitable periods by the surplus profit created during profitable periods. An eight-hour workday that creates profit lets you rest the sixteen other hours. A parent that produces profit means their children don't have to work.

If the farmer and food manufacturer don't produce a profit, there's no food to distribute as food stamps. The attempt to distribute first and profit second was attempted by Stalin, and led to the starvation of seven million people in Ukraine. Not a good strategy.

Capitalism and the Industrial Revolution have made this simple mechanism happen on a global scale.

Wealth was created by generating profit through repurposing existing resources into higher and better uses.

Economists refer to this as productivity, and the gains made in productivity over the past century have been tremendous. The average workweek is shorter and yet living standards are higher. It would take the average American only eleven hours of labor per week to produce as much as he or she could have produced in forty hours in 1950.

This is not to say profit cures all woes. There are a lot of considerations to take into account, like the justice and happiness of living in a highly unequal, albeit profitable society.

However, the premise remains true: profit always comes first. Before we debate over how to divvy up the pie, we must first bake it.

Now that we've established that getting rich is a good thing, let's talk about the best ways to bake some pie.

JOBS (THE SLOW LANE) VS. ENTREPRENEURSHIP (THE FAST LANE)

Raised by a single, working class mother, MJ Demarco dreamed of getting rich. Neither physically gifted nor born with some innate talent that would lead him to superstardom, MJ didn't see a path to getting rich other than the 30-year trudge up the corporate ladder many face today.

MJ recounts going out for an ice cream as a teenager in suburban Chicago. Approaching the ice cream parlor, he saw a Lamborghini Countach parked outside. The Countach, the ultimate symbol of success in young MJ's mind, was piloted not by an old corporate tycoon, but a young man in his late 20s or early 30s.

How could he afford a car like that so young?

Seizing his chance, MJ stopped the young man sliding into his car.

"What do you do?"

Briefly pausing, the Countach owner turned to MJ and replied: "I'm an inventor."

His encounter with Countach set MJ off on a quest to find young people that were rich and figure out how they got there.

Years later, after selling his company and buying his own Lamborghini, MJ authored *The Millionaire Fastlane,* where he breaks down two primary financial roadmaps to wealth.

1. The slow lane in the form of jobs, a path that most people raised in our society see.

2. The fast lane, entrepreneurship, the path most people don't see and one that's becoming easier, safer, and more profitable.

JOBS: THE SLOW LANE

The slow lane is embodied by the concept of "get rich slowly" and is the doctrine of most people we consider financially responsible today.

The recipe is well-known: find a stable job, pay off debt, put 10% into the market, and watch it compound over time.

It's the belief that the path to getting wealthy is to work 60 hours a week for the next 40 years at one or perhaps a few different jobs.

It's typified by spreadsheets most financial planners use to show the compound interest of saving 10% each year and having that compound 10% over time.

Stated in a formula:

Wealth = Job + Market Investments

If we factor that, it ends up being expressed:

Wealth = Intrinsic Value + Compound Interest

Let's break that down.

The Two Limits of Intrinsic Value

> *Jobs suck because they're rooted in limited leverage and limited control. Sure, you can have great job (and a fun one too!) but in the scope of wealth, they limit both leverage and control—two things desperately needed if you want wealth.*[48]
>
> – MJ DEMARCO

The most important thing to understand about intrinsic value is this: jobs are fundamentally linked to time. Whether you make $500k per year or $8 per hour, your earning capacity at a job is linked to your time.

This is essential because time is the only truly limited resource in the universe. As the Industrial Revolution proved, we can make more money and more wealth. We still haven't invented the ability to make more time. Because you can only make more money by investing more time, we have no leverage to accelerate how much we earn beyond simply working more and more, which is exactly what most people have done.

Whether you want to be Scrooge-McDuck-swimming-in-piles-of-money rich or you just want to make enough money to provide a good lifestyle and have time to pursue other hobbies, be it exotic travel or raising your kids, you can't do this as long as your income is linked to your time.

What's more and more often overlooked: you give up control. You can't make decisions outside the scope of your job. If external market forces doom the company, they doom you as well.

Let's say you're a journalist. You are working at the *Chronicle* newspaper in a city where the *Journal* newspaper is the leader. As traditional print media is consolidating and many secondary or tertiary papers are going out of business, it doesn't matter how good of a journalist you are. You're going to lose your job and the paper is going to go under. You've abdicated control.

Sure, you could go get a job at another newspaper, but what happens in five years when that newspaper is put out of business by an online publication? You're stuck in a cycle of limited control.

This is the angle of jobs many people don't see: they don't do a very good job of protecting their downside. Jobs were safe in a world where more and more were being created and wages were increasing—which they were for most of the 20th century. Since around 1980, that hasn't been the case. It certainly hasn't been the case this century as population growth has outpaced job growth at a rate of 2.4 times since 2000.

I was speaking with a mid-twenties male recently who is at a well-known, prestigious law school. He'd just received an offer from a well-known law firm in New York City. For someone coming out of school, this is as good an outcome as can be expected. He related to me that most people put in three to seven years after law school, during which they are able to pay off their debt by working 80–100 hours a week. At the end of those three to seven years, they will either make partner or choose to go to another firm with better work/life balance.

This is broadly considered a safe and profitable choice. He certainly thought so. His parents thought so as well.

In the firm he was going to work for, an entire generation of lawyers was passed over for partnership because they came of age right at the 2008 financial crisis. For factors outside their control, they had no ability to protect their downside.

Jobs not only limit the upside of intrinsic value by tying money to time—they also give up control. We have no leverage beyond trading more time, which is our most valuable and only truly limited asset. We lose control to react to market forces outside the scope of the job.

ENTREPRENEURSHIP: THE FAST LANE

The alternative to jobs, entrepreneurship, is based on Fast Lane math. At its core is a focus on rapidly building assets that grow without perpetually requiring direct intervention.

According to research and marketing firm The Harrison Group (**HarrisonGroupInc.com**), only 10% of penta-millionaires (net worth $5 million) report that their wealth came from passive investments.[49]

They accumulated their wealth actively through building businesses, assets that grew without them. I spoke with a business owner who had a similar experience to MJ. He'd always loved cars and spent time at the race track growing up. He had a moment of realization when he saw that the only way he could ever race consistently was if he became an entrepreneur.

In order to race cars, you need lots of money and lots of time. While a high-paying job in finance may get you the former and a beach bum lifestyle may get you the latter, it was only entrepreneurs that had both money and time.

Stated in a formula, the Fast Lane is:

Wealth = Net Profit + Asset Value

Those terms are defined:

Net Profit = (Units Sold) × (Unit Profit)

Asset Value = (Net Profit) × (Industry Multiplier)

Let's start with the first equation: net profit. Net profit, commonly called profit, just means the profit left after we've accounted for all expenses and costs of delivering a product.

Increasing Net Profit: Controllable, Unlimited Variables Make You Rich

The first essential element to understand here is that of the unlimited upside. In a job, your upside is always limited. But look at The Portable Bar Company again (the business I worked with that sold portable bars). Over the course of 18 months, just a year and a half, the business grew by 527%.

Most self-funded startups, entrepreneurs, and businesses I work with and talk with are disappointed by 20% annual growth in the business, while most people with jobs I know are grateful to get their 3% annual cost of living raise.

Because they have unlimited control and unlimited variables, exponential growth is possible.

We can understand this better by using author and marketer Perry Marshall's Traffic, Economics, Conversion triangle. By increasing any one of the factors above, we can increase the amount of money the business generates.[50]

Traffic Economics

The Tactical Triangle

A. Traffic—Sell more units by increasing Traffic

B. Economics—Raise Unit Profit

C. Conversions—Sell more units by increasing the Conversion Ratio

Raising any one of these variables will increase the amount of net profit the business generates.

In the case of the Portable Bar Company, we increased traffic to the website by 289% over the course of 18 months using paid advertising from Google Adwords and content marketing.

Then we doubled the value of a visitor by improving our conversion rate with tactics like email marketing and retargeting campaigns.

Then we improved the economics by designing and selling new product lines with better profit margins.

If you have a new, more profitable product available, the likelihood of a visitor buying it increases. You're more likely to have what they are looking for since the product line is bigger. The value of each visitor increases.

Because the new product has higher margins, it also returns more net profit, giving you more money to reinvest into the business and further increase traffic, conversions, or design new products. Increasing traffic or conversions also increases word-of-mouth marketing down the line, as more customers means more discussion about your products. As more people becomes customers, you have more word-of-mouth marketing since more people have your products to talk about.

The end result is that all of these factors, fully under your control, begin to compound. More people come to the site. Of those, a higher percentage of them buy, and on average, they buy more expensive items. While raising any one of these variables increases the net profit of the business, raising all of them at the same time results in dramatic growth.

Unlike a job, there is no ceiling. While you can certainly tap out an industry and exhaust demand there, you will have acquired resources that you can use to invest in another industry, exactly what Rob Walling and other entrepreneurs did by stair stepping their way into better and better businesses.

Many entrepreneurs now release income reports showing their businesses growth.

Dan Norris and Alex McClafferty founded WP Curve in 2012, and are on pace to do $768,000 in 2015.

John Lee Dumas has gone from never having run a business in 2010 to over $100,000 in monthly revenue in October 2013 and $433,000 in monthly revenue in February 2015.

Buffer, a web application, has grown from less than $130,000 in monthly revenue in September 2013 to over $300,000 in August 2014.

Groove HQ, another software application, has grown from $35,000 in monthly revenue to over $75,000 in less than a year.

Am I cherry-picking the best examples here? Definitely. The guys with slower growth aren't broadcasting their slow growth for us to look at. The point is that it's possible to grow at these rates. In a job, it's not.

As you invest more in entrepreneurship and become a better entrepreneur, this becomes easier and easier. Because you're building a skill set around entrepreneurship, your first company may not hit these kinds of numbers, but you can stair step your way into something like this.

Assets Are More Valuable Than Cash

Every dollar you add to the bottom line of a business is actually increased by a multiple.

Unlike a job where your income is simply cash, net profit is actually the number used to value your business as an asset.

While multiples vary across industry and not all businesses can be sold, almost all businesses can be designed to sell if you ever decide to.

If your business has a 2× multiple, a conservative number—most businesses are worth more than that—the business is worth twice the net profit in generates.

Let's say you're in a job and you get a big raise, an extra $50,000 more per year.

That's pretty sweet right? You can do a lot with an extra $50,000.

Let's say you do the same in a business you own by generating an extra $50,000 in profit. You add not only $50,000 to your pocket, but also $100,000 in asset value to your net worth because of the multiple.

Unlike a raise, adding $50,000 in profit to your company's bottom line increases the value of the asset, which you own.

Imagine getting a $50,000 raise and then having a free $100,000 thrown in.

That's effectively what happens when an entrepreneur adds $50,000 in net profit to their business.

The multiples that are commanded by entrepreneurial companies when they're acquired by corporations are seemingly absurd, and yet steadily rising.

Entrepreneurial companies that were acquired in the last five years like Mint, WhatsApp, and Oculus Rift all got multiples far higher than what any traditional business valuation would have yielded because they positioned themselves to be strategically acquired. Less than two years after it was founded, Oculus Rift was bought by Facebook for $2 billion. WhatsApp was also acquired by Facebook for $21.8 billion, 2000× the annual revenue. Financial tracking company Mint was bought by Intuit two years after it was founded for $170 million.

While these companies are certainly outliers, the phenomenon is true on a smaller scale as well. I've spoken with dozens of business brokers selling smaller companies in the five- to seven-figure range and none of them can keep up with the demand from buyers in small, growing companies.

Business brokers are awash in buyers and almost desperately looking for sellers.

Both of these phenomena support exactly what we keep seeing: the scarce resource is entrepreneurship and individuals with money and capital have realized this, and are willing to invest far more in entrepreneurs and what they create, than in employees.

Laura, an entrepreneur I spoke with recently, has been running her business for a little less than ten years. The business currently generates mid six figures in profit and has, since its inception, grown at a rate of over 50% per year. The business is run with around ten hours of work from Laura each week.

How many people do you know that, ten years into their job, are earning mid six figures, working less than ten hours per week, and own an asset worth over $1 million if they chose to sell it?

It's cheaper, easier, and safer to start a business. When you grow it using variables you control, you make more money because you have unlimited leverage. You also are building an asset which can be sold. And, you've acquired a skillset that protects your downside.

Compound Interest Is Valuable Once You Have a Lot of Money

Oft-revered for their investing prowess, Warren Buffett and Charlie Munger of Berkshire Hathaway love to preach the value of compound interest. Relatively small percentages compounded over time can add up to the billions that Buffett and Munger have managed to accumulate over their careers as investors.

While there's a tremendous amount to learn from individuals like Buffett and Munger, it's worth considering their perspective. Compound interest on "float" (the money currently in their insurance businesses from paid premiums until claims are paid it out) is powerful for them because they are compounding *billions* of dollars.

If you have $10 million and lend it out at a 5% interest rate then you'd be getting $41,666 in passive income every month. That's without ever touching the principal $10 million sitting in the bank. Not bad.

One Penny Doubled

Years	Amount	Years	Amount
Age 21	.01	Age 41	10,485.76
Age 22	.02	Age 42	20,971.52
Age 23	.04	Age 43	41,943.04
Age 24	.08	Age 44	83,886.08
Age 25	.16	Age 45	167,772.16
Age 26	.32	Age 46	335,544.32
Age 27	.64	Age 47	671,088.64
Age 28	1.28	Age 48	1,342,177.28
Age 29	2.56	Age 49	2,684,354.56
Age 30	5.12	Age 50	5,368,709.12
Age 31	10.24	Age 51	10,737,418.24
Age 32	20.48	Age 52	21,474,836.48
Age 33	40.96	Age 53	42,949,672.96
Age 34	81.92	Age 54	85,899,345.92
Age 35	163.84	Age 55	171,798,691.84
Age 36	327.68	Age 56	343,597,383.68
Age 37	655.36	Age 57	687,194,767.36
Age 38	1,310.72	Age 58	1,374,389,534.72
Age 39	2,621.44	Age 59	2,748,779,069.44
Age 40	5,242.88	Age 60	5,497,558,138.88

Can You Bypass 30 Years and Start Here?

If you build a company and sell it for a few million dollars, then compound interest is powerful.

While the math and logic behind the Fast Lane vs. Slow Lane has always been true, the internet and economic changes we've discussed have made the entrepreneurial path more accessible and the potential gains larger.

EXPECTED VALUE: WHY A LOT OF FORMER POKER PLAYERS ARE ENTREPRENEURS

A disproportionately large number of poker players end up becoming entrepreneurs.

Now I see why: they get the math.

When it comes to the way systems and probabilities work in the modern world, our intuition is poor to say the least.

Just as many amateurs see poker as a game of luck, many non-entrepreneurs see entrepreneurial success as luck. They think people that have prosperous businesses just got lucky and were "overnight successes." They don't see the years or decades of work, skill acquisition, and relationships that the entrepreneurs built up.

They also typically haven't been exposed to a simple, yet powerful concept: *expected value.*

Professional poker players are remarkably consistent in their earnings. What looks random from the amateur's perspective is, from the professional's angle, quite predictable.

It's normal for poker players to lose a hand worth thousands of dollars, but be happy with how they played it. They understood what the probabilities were and bet accordingly.

Imagine that you're playing a hand with one remaining card to be shown. You have to pay $1,000 to see the final card and stay in the hand. You know there is a 20% chance that it will be the card you need and you will win the entire hand worth $20,000.

If you pay $1,000, then you have a 20% chance to win $20,000. That is, you pay $1,000 for an *expected value* of $4,000 (20% × $20,000 = $4,000).

If it isn't the card you need, that's unfortunate. But, it doesn't mean you shouldn't have bet the way you did. If you were faced with that same situation one hundred times and bet the same each time, you would obviously invest. The large number of instances would make it all but certain that in sum, you would come out ahead. Paying $1000 to get $4000 is a straightforward proposition.

Expected Value is the sum of all possible values for a random variable, each value multiplied by its probability of occurrence. It's what poker players use to make betting decisions and it's how entrepreneurs think about their businesses and decisions.

Billy Murphy, a former professional poker player turned entrepreneur, explains a scenario that a prospective entrepreneur might face in his essay *Expected Value: Millionaire's Math*.

Suppose you have $30,000 saved up and are debating between getting a job or starting a commerce store. You could simply evaluate the expected value of each.

The typical way someone approaches this might be: "If I get a job, I can make $50,000/year. If I start a store I could potentially make more, but it's also risky." They never specifically quantify the outcomes, leading to poor decisions.

Let's apply some numbers. If you go out and get a job, you may make $50,000, but if you start a store, the expected value may be $95,000 based on industry averages of estimated earnings and the added value of the asset, because all profits of a business you own are worth a multiple. Unlike a job, a business has potentially unlimited upside and you control the variables.

If the store doesn't work out, then you have $30,000 in living expenses which will still cover you for 15 months until you'd need to find a job. If the store starts to make money, that will buy you more time.

As soon as you quantify the outcomes, it changes the decision. Even if the expected value option doesn't pan out, you can always go back to the job. The worst case scenario is you've acquired a valuable new skillset to put on your resume.

While no individual opportunity is guaranteed to pan out, systematically pursuing opportunities with a positive expected value means you're going to find success over time.[51]

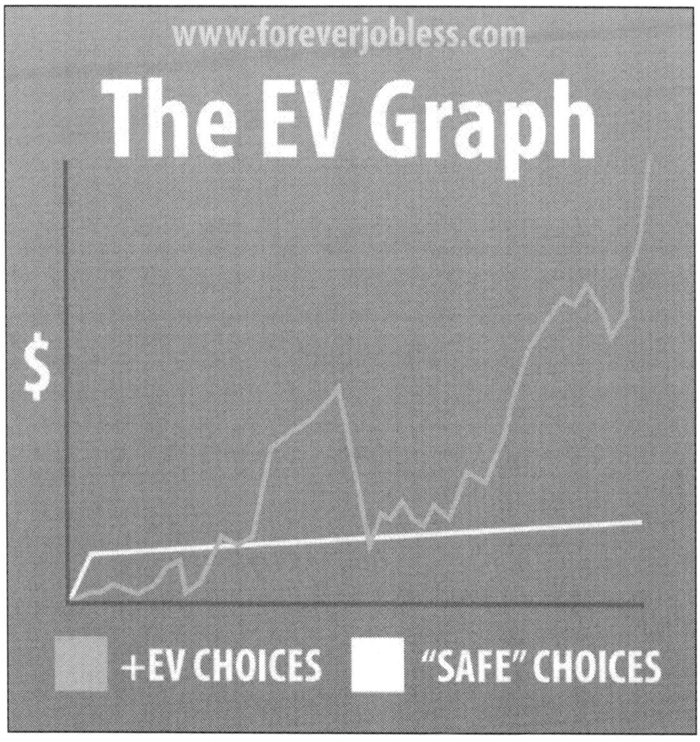

This is key to understanding the sensibility of entrepreneurship as a career choice. While any individual business opportunity may fail, the systematic pursuit of opportunities that are positive expected value is more likely to pan out.

Scott Adams, the creator of the *Dilbert* comic, frequently cites over a dozen failed businesses he launched other than *Dilbert*, now one of the most widely syndicated comics in the world, and one that's made Adams worth over $75 million. While he's had many failed ventures, the success of *Dilbert* more than compensates.

While the math behind EV has always been true, it's now even more true because entrepreneurship is radically more accessible, the downside is dramatically lower, and potential upside is higher.

Dan Norris failed at 83% of the businesses that he launched in 2014, but the success of WP Curve more than made up for all those failures.

Because the internet and technology have democratized product creation and distribution, you don't have to invest tens of thousands of dollars or years of time on each opportunity. Instead of having to open a store on Main St., sign a lease for thousands of dollars, and pay thousands of dollars in advertising media, you can write posts on a blog (a few hundred dollars at most to set up a website) and then launch a new business in a week.

You also expect some outcomes to dwarf other outcomes. In Extremistan, this is to be expected. Because the internet exposes entrepreneurs to potentially huge markets, there is more upside than ever before.

CHAPTER 12

MORE FREEDOM

Work as Choice, Not Work as Obligation

"There is only one success—to be able to spend your life in your own way."

– CHRISTOPHER MORLEY

"Upon graduation, my primary driver was freedom. I remember thinking that at the time. I would like to be anywhere, anytime I wanted and have a lot of money."

– DAN ANDREWS

Across time periods, across cultures, across genders, there are no lines that a desire for freedom hasn't crossed.

Why do we want to be free?

That's not clear.

However, the phenomenology that every individual fights to exercise a greater degree of freedom in their life is crystal clear.

We, as a species and individuals, always want freedom. Once we get it, we always want more.

HOW TO HAVE A LOWER ACCEPTANCE RATE THAN HARVARD

Over the past two hundred years, since the dawn of the Industrial Revolution, the amount of wealth available in the world has increased dramatically. Even as the population has gone from 978 million to over seven billion, the GDP per capita has gone from $300 to over $20,000 in Western democracies. We've had a population explosion, but the increase in wealth hasn't just kept pace—it's raced ahead.

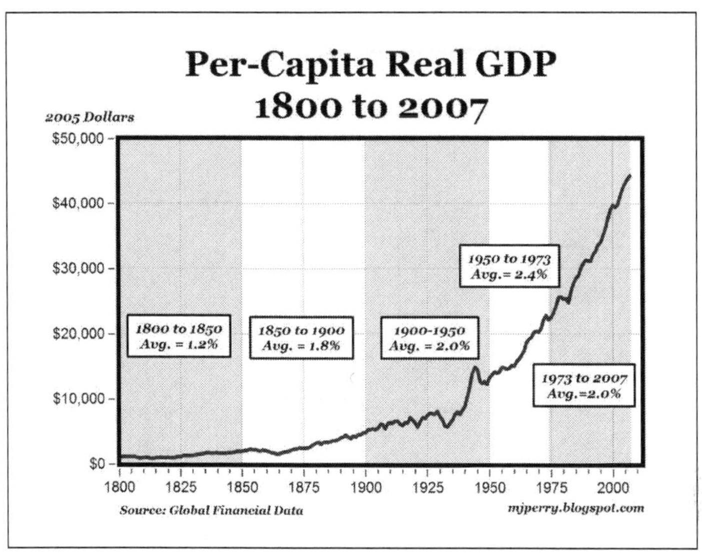

http://mjperry.blogspot.ca/2011/02/caplan-and-lindsey-and-very-slight.html

Whether on an individual level or a societal level, as we have more and more access to resources, we have to choose what to do with them. It's clear that one of the ways we choose to allocate that wealth is towards a greater expression of freedom.

It's common for people to take significant salary cuts to move into flexible or remote work arrangements. Presented with a clear cut case between more money and more freedom, they opt for more freedom.

I spent two years working with a small entrepreneurial company starting in a position that, at the time, meant a 50% pay cut, and a demotion from project management to grunt work.

When I told my former boss I was leaving, he came back

the next day and said he wanted to make me a counter offer, including a raise. I walked, because I wanted two things that it was next to impossible for him to provide given his company's structure: freedom and meaning in the work.

I wanted the freedom to travel, to work when and where I wanted, to leverage my best energy and best work.

The company I was going to work for ran a publishing business that has since grown into the one from the introduction, now hosting conferences and meetups around the world.

I had been reading their blog and listening to their podcast for over two years at that point, and I resonated with how they ran their company. I bought into the mission behind the company hook, line, and sinker. I believed in "building businesses to create more freedom and wealth in your life and the lives of those you love."

The way they ran the company reflected it. They plowed excess profits back into the company, which enabled them to create more freedom and wealth in their lives, the lives of their team, and the lives of their customers.

That company has a substantially lower acceptance rate than Harvard for new applicants to an entry level position.

Escape The City is a job board founded by three ex-corporate employees targeted at highly successful corporate types and lawyers. I've seen hundreds of applications come from highly educated, affluent individuals fighting for an opportunity to dump their six-figure corporate salary for an entry level one that dramatically cuts their salary, but gives them more freedom and meaning in their work.

THE SILENT REVOLUTION OF THE 20TH CENTURY

Over time, as the West has advanced and more wealth has been created, more and more people have claimed that wealth in the form of freedom. Remote working may be the latest incarnation, but it's certainly not the first.

Martin Luther led the Protestant Revolution, which gave substantially more freedom to Christians compared to the Catholic Church. The freedom to interpret religious scripture was no longer left to a single man, but distributed to individuals.

The Founding Fathers of the U.S.—Jefferson, Franklin, and Washington, among others—led the American Revolution, creating the first republic government in the Modern West. This gave more freedom to more individuals than the Parliamentary monarchy they had previously suffered.

What has gone quietly unremarked upon in history books is that the 20th century marked the greatest expansion of freedom in human history. The emergence of the modern middle class in liberal democracies during the 20th century led to more people acquiring more freedom than in all of history up to that point.

The Founding Fathers distributed power from a monarch and a parliament to a group of rich, white landowners. From a few hundred to a few thousand. It was, at the time, revolutionary. It sparked and inspired a wave of democratic revolutions over the next century.

Yet, the level of freedom enjoyed by the average middle class individual in the West today is beyond the wildest imagination of anyone alive in the 19th, much less 18th, century.

FREER THAN JOHN D.

The Baby Boomer generation built the knowledge economy, which gave them more free time and the discretionary income to enjoy it than their parents' generation ever imagined.

At work, what they think about requires problem-solving and creative thinking. Unlike the mass of factory and agricultural workers a hundred years ago, the bulk of the middle class today is engaged in knowledge work, more interesting and stimulating than cog work in mass manufacturing.

At home, they have freedom to pursue hobbies and the free time to do so. The average work week dropped from almost eighty hours a week in the late 19th century to around forty in the mid-20th century, where it's hovered since.

The average middle class worker in liberal democracies of the West today is freer in how and where they spend their best energy and time than John D. Rockefeller was one hundred years ago when he was among the ten richest men on Earth. The guy in his mid-30s that lives in the apartment next door is freer than John D., the industrial titan, was a century ago.

Modern communication technology alone would let him bring down Standard Oil in it's heyday. The internet and technology we've developed over the last century all enable entirely new dimensions of freedom that Rockefeller couldn't have imagined.

The insider information he used to gain key advantages for Standard Oil during its rise would be entirely undercut by a iPhone with a Stocks app installed.

If you own a Kindle and a smart phone, you have access to more books and knowledge than Rockefeller could have even imagined possible, much less had access to himself.

Ideas and concepts which never even entered Rockefeller's consciousness are now almost ubiquitous. The rise in Zen Buddhism and Stoic philosophy in the modern West is closely linked to the rise of technology and the internet. Rockefeller simply never had access to those ideas despite having enough money to buy a small country.

Rockefeller only left the United States once in his life. Getting on a boat is an affair. Getting on a plane is an afternoon. You can buy a roundtrip ticket to Europe for less than $1000.

He spent days riding trains between his expensive summer homes and the Standard Oil office in New York.

We spend hours riding planes between AirBnB apartments. A level of freedom that cost him millions to create can be recreated today for a few hundred.

Rockefeller, as opposed to his contemporaries, was incredibly free. Compared with a typical Standard Oil employee, Rockefeller enjoyed a level of autonomy and freedom in his time and location that was unprecedented one hundred years ago. Most Standard Oil employees never left their state, much less their country.

For much of the middle class, the level of freedom Rockefeller enjoyed is now taken for granted.

This natural desire for increasing amounts of freedom has been one of the main drivers in the advancement of civilization.

We've gone from one man, Luther; to a small group of men, the Founding Fathers; to a whole segment of society, the middle class Baby Boomer generation. And in each case, not only has the size of the group increased, but so too has their degree of freedom. The professional middle class individual today has far more freedom than John D.

DESIGN > CHOICE

Who has the power in a republic like the U.S.? Who is the most free? The obvious answer would be the voters, right?

Not quite.

The people who *really* have power are those who decide which candidates show up on the voters' ballots. They're able to create the options you choose from.

In reality, there are a nearly infinite number of ideological choices for president or senator, but we get stuck in a Republican/Democrat paradigm because that's what we see as citizens and voters.

Our role there is not to design, but to choose from a set of options designed for us.

In a world of vast possibilities, we focus all our attention on a relatively tiny portion because the most powerful people are structuring the consciousness of everyone else.

The power in a republic is more dispersed than in a monarchy, but it isn't totally free.

One way our generation has fought to distribute freedom and to gain more if it can be seen in the culture around protesting through movements like Occupy Wall Street. They appeal to the people that do have power in the hopes they'll be "fair" or "just."

Regardless of what is fair or just, what the protestors are missing is that we, today, our generation, have more opportunity not to ask for power, but to wrest it from the structures that exist.

Companies like AirBnB didn't ask for power from Hilton—they

leveraged the technology and the internet to take it. This happens on much smaller scales as well.

If our generation chooses it, if we seize it, the degree of freedom we can create is beyond the capability of human imagination. It's entirely possible that the freedom you can create in your life within two decades will be beyond the imagination of many people alive today.

Instead of choosing from a set of available options, we can create our own. It's the triumph of design over choice. Instead of ordering from the menu, we are more empowered than any prior generation to become the cooks.

ARE YOU STRUCTURING YOUR REALITY OR HAVING IT STRUCTURED FOR YOU?

Where do you fall on this line?

Least free ——————————————————————Most Free
Industrial——————————Knowledge——————————Entrepreneurial
Follow Rulebook————Assign Others to Follow Rulebook—————Design Rulebook

The least free are those whose reality is structured for them. "Stay tuned," they are told before each *Jeopardy* commercial break, and they do so. At work they are assigned tasks and roles that are clearly defined. They exert very little freedom over their reality.

The middle class has created a greater degree of independence and structure a greater deal of their own realities. They are more likely to structure their families and hobbies in ways they find more meaningful and not just as the mass media may instruct them. At work they are likely to do things which require solving more complex problems and defining tasks for others.

But the most powerful are those who design both their own realities and the realities of others. They write the TV shows and design the products that the masses consume. The entrepreneur defines reality, he is not defined by it. He is engaged in a dialogue with his reality asking "why" and "why not" instead of "how" or "what." [52]

The degree to which we're able to design our reality is directly related to our quality of life, freedom, and wealth. Those that design reality have a higher quality of all factors in their life, and through designing their reality they enable others to do the same by creating more wealth. In designing my reality in the form of an iPhone, Steve Jobs and Apple created more power, freedom, and wealth for me than Rockefeller had. This leads to an upward spiral. As wealth is increasing, so is our ability to design our realities.

PHD OR PODCAST?

While it's always been true that great work comes from those who freely choose it and that the ability to design our realities creates more freedom, it's the changes we've seen over the past decade that made both of those radically more accessible and safer.

Dan Andrews had a passion for reading books and exploring interesting ideas. Leaving school, he faced the choice between going into business and entrepreneurship and going into academia as a PhD. Given those interests, most people would have advised him to get a PhD.

Let's look at the realities of those two paths. A good scenario for a Philosophy PhD is investing seven to ten years in getting the degree. Because academia has become so competitive, Dan would have considered himself lucky to end up on a tenure track at a middle-of-the-road university. If he did manage to land a tenure position, he would spend twenty hours per week teaching classes, twenty hours per week grading papers, and twenty hours per week managing administration.

He wouldn't get to start reading the books and exploring the ideas he got into academia for in the first place until sixty hours into his week.

Instead, Dan chose to go into business. He now hosts a weekly podcast where he explores the ideas in books he's read and uses them to help other entrepreneurs grow their businesses. Unlike a professor, he's not playing politics to decide what he can or can't publish. He has the freedom to explore the ideas he wants to in the way that he wants to, unburdened by internal politics.

In much the same way that the average middle class individual today is freer than John D. Rockefeller was a century ago, a self-described middle-of-the-road entrepreneur is freer to actually do Philosophy than a tenured Philosophy professor and create a bigger impact in the process.

The difference between Dan and a PhD is that Dan didn't choose any of the options available to him—he created one, he found a better leverage point.[53]

Rob Walling described running his company in much the same way: "I am so much more in control. I have freedom in where I live. I have freedom of my time. I can decide what to do and when to do it. I don't really have a boss. And, to a degree, I have income freedom, I can work harder and make more money." [54]

A SLIGHTLY BETTER BLACKBERRY

What's the source of this phenomenon? Why is it that more freedom and autonomy creates even more freedom and autonomy?

Edward Deci, the founder of Self-determination theory, noticed in his experiments and observations that great work emerged when individuals had more freedom, and were, in a sense, allowed to be more entrepreneurial.

If we think of the great contributions made to human society, they were all made by people that were free to do whatever they wanted, but used the freedom to create.

Vincent Van Gogh wasn't obligated to paint; he freely chose it. He struggled early in his life seeking work:

> *"One of the reasons why I'm now without a position, why I've been without a position for years, it's quite simply because I have different ideas from these gentlemen who give positions to individuals who think like them."*

Imagine someone telling Steve Jobs that he had to design a new phone. Given that sense of obligation, he likely would have just made a slightly better Blackberry.

Great work—the kind of work that will create wealth in our lives and the lives of others is not the product of obligation—is the product of freedom. Freedom gives us a longer lever, a better leverage point.

By seeking more freedom and building it into our lives, we not only improve our ability to create more material wealth and make more money personally, but we also create more of it in the world at large.

CHAPTER 13

MORE MEANING

The Final Key to Wealth

> *"I think when people are dancing on the edge of failure and they're growing and there's a void over there, but they keep moving forward, that's when we feel alive as people."*
>
> – SETH GODIN, STARTUP SCHOOL

I stood in a friend's backyard, shoulder aching and sore, hands almost totally numb. She'd gone out to a movie with her husband and I'd volunteered to watch their son.

Her son, who had recently been diagnosed by teachers as being "incapable of paying attention," spent three hours with me in the backyard running routes and incessantly asking me questions about football.

"Why do some players start with their hands down on the ground and others start standing?"

"Is it more important to be fast or quick if you want to be a receiver in the NFL?"

"Why are more teams moving to the spread formation?"

"How do they know if the QB is going to throw it over their inside shoulder or outside shoulder?"

After three hours of rapid fire questions and practice, his parents came back. I drove home exhausted. He was still bursting with energy.

He had just spent 3 hours learning and growing as a football player, something that was deeply important to him. He hadn't switched tasks every five minutes; at no point had he wanted to jump into something else.

Incapable of paying attention indeed. Perhaps it wasn't that he couldn't pay attention, but that sitting at a desk for eight hours a day staring at a whiteboard isn't intention-inducing.

WHAT DRIVES US?

In his seminal work, *Flow*, psychologist Mihaly Csikszentmihalyi presents decades of his own research on man's search for happiness and personal growth.

Happiness, he explains, isn't just something that happens. We can't buy it with money or command it to happen no matter how much power we have. It doesn't depend on outside events, but our interpretation of them. Happiness is a condition which can be prepared for and cultivated. It's that ability to control our own inner experience that will determine the quality of our lives.

We cultivate happiness through seeking what Csikszentmihalyi calls *flow*. *Flow*, at its essence, is the ultimate natural expression of the human desire to grow and stretch.

Flow is the moment of struggling and reaching out your hand for a goal to overcome a challenge. When asked to cite the most enjoyable moment of their lives, people usually recall these moments—the challenge of raising a child or helping build a company.

A person who is chasing consciously chosen goals can't help but grow into a deeper, more complex individual. It's in stretching skills, reaching up for higher challenges, that we become increasingly complex and more capable individuals and, consequently, more valuable to the marketplace.

Think back to the moments in your life where you remember being the happiest. What were the moments where you were working on something only to look up and realize hours had flown by? When time whizzed by in a blur because you were so immersed in the work.

These are moments of Flow.

Edward Deci's research supports Csikszentmihalyi's conclusions. Deci believed that we, as humans, have an "inherent tendency to seek out novelty and challenges, to extend and exercise their capacities, to explore, and to learn."

There is, however, a catch to Deci's theory.

"One who is interested in developing and enhancing intrinsic motivation in children, employees, students, etc. should not concentrate on external-control systems such as monetary rewards," he wrote in a follow-up paper.[55]

That is, when we treat work as jobs, as an obligation, a disutility, something that has to be balanced, the inherent tendency to grow breaks down.

Deci and Csikszentmihalyi are joined by Frederick Herzberg, a psychologist cum management consultant who proposed two key factors describing work performance. The first was a basic handling of hygiene factors such as enough money and job security. This was the baseline necessary to present dissatisfaction or unhappiness with work. If someone is worried about making ends meet or paying rent, they won't have a lot of creativity to spread around.

But to create truly remarkable work, the most important factors were the same intrinsic factors cited by Deci and Csikszentmihalyi.

W. Edwards Deming made the same argument in his work with Japanese firms, advocating creating more intrinsic motivation as the route to quality and continual improvement. His work, which was eventually brought over to America in the form of kaizen (or continuous improvement), created billions of dollars in value for companies around the world.[56]

What Deming, Deci, Herzberg, and Csikszentmihalyi all found can be summed up in two statements:

1. We are naturally predisposed to be growing, goal-seeking, striving creatures.

2. By following that impulse we can create more valuable work.

When we spend our time striving and growing towards a task that we freely choose, we do better work. The same input creates more input. We have a longer lever.

It's in the moments of searching and striving for those goals that we find *flow*. It's in the entrepreneurial search for something more, for seeking and striving, that people do their best work.

A study which looked at the work of 11,000 industrial scientists and engineers working in U.S. based companies confirms the urge to master something new and engaging was the best predictor of productivity. Scientists motivated by an intrinsic desire filed significantly more patents than those whose main motivation was money, even if we control for the amount of effort each group put in.[57]

A natural drive towards an intellectual challenge resulted in more innovation and more patents. This is counterintuitive to how most people view motivation and work. We assume that paying people more will yield better work. And with good reason: for the last few thousand years, it's been true.

SIMPLE, ALGORITHMIC VS. COMPLEX, HEURISTIC WORK

For centuries, traditional motivators have been effective: good pay, discipline, and direction. They let Alexander the Great reach India and they enabled John Rockefeller to build his industrial empire.

But do they still motivate us?

Pay is certainly a motivator to the extent that it's necessary for acquiring a certain level of lifestyle or wealth. If you aren't going to make rent or be able to eat, money certainly motivates. But money gets people from nothing to something. Discipline and direction serve in much the same way. For someone that has no direction or no discipline, they're typically beneficial. Many people who struggled with drug addiction or other destabilizing life conditions cite working in organizations like Starbucks, which has strict discipline and direction, as something that got them back on track.

That kind of motivation serves an important role for some people, but it doesn't generally create great work.

Predictably Irrational author Dan Ariely, along with three other economists in Madurai, India, conducted an illuminating experiment on the power of incentives. The quartet of economists assigned participants work that could be subdivided into heuristic and algorithmic work.

Algorithmic work is anything where a simple formula can be used; it's work that falls into the simple domain. Imagine an assembly line or putting together a piece of furniture. Each task clearly follows the next. Algorithmic work isn't particularly scarce or valuable. It's also not very fun, which is why paying more for it works. If you're slogging through something rote you don't want to do, then rationalizing it with a big payout works. When Henry Ford increased the pay of his factory workers in 1905, he got better performance out of them. A worker on an assembly line doesn't require a lot of creativity or innovation.

A computer program is simply a complex algorithm. Google, a $380 billion dollar company, is built on its proprietary search algorithm. By definition, algorithmic work is the simple work that is going to be replaced by machines and outsourcing in the near future.

Heuristic work, work where there may be guidelines but not hard and fast rules, is qualitatively different; it's work that falls closer to the complex domain. There isn't one way to grow a business or paint a portrait. There are heuristics and guidelines around it, but you can employ different methods and still be successful.

Different businesses in the same industry can use different

marketing plans and still be successful. Heuristic work, unlike algorithmic work, is scarce and valuable. It can't easily be outsourced and it can't be made into a computer program. It's the kind of work done by entrepreneurs and entrepreneurial individuals inside companies.

Because they performed the experiment in India, the scientists were able to offer a relatively big financial incentive. For completing a complex, heuristic task, one group was offered a small reward (equivalent to one day's wage), a second group was offered a medium reward (equivalent to two weeks' wage) and a third group was offered a large reward (equivalent to five months' wage).

Based on how we traditionally understand the role of incentives, we would expect that each group's performance would increase as the monetary reward increased.

For heuristic, complex tasks, the results of the experiment were precisely the opposite.

Going from one day to two weeks' pay in reward didn't improve performance at all. Going from two weeks to five months' decreased performance.[58] As the pay increased, the group did worse at more complex tasks like unscrambling the anagram. Being purely incentivized by money reduced the quality of the work and made it less valuable.

In another experiment where researchers looked at artists, they found that the work was actually worse when they were doing it as a job as opposed to something they choose to do.

> *"Our results were quite startling. The commissioned (**read: job-based**) works were rated as significantly less creative than the non-commissioned (**read: entrepreneurial**) works, yet they were not rated as different in technical quality. Moreover, the artists reported feeling significantly more constrained when doing commissioned works than when doing non-commissioned works."*

An artist interviewed following a separate, similar experiment testing the interplay of creativity and incentives said, "Not always, but a lot of the time, when you are doing a piece for someone else it becomes more 'work' than joy. When I work for myself there is the pure joy of creating and I can work through the night and not even know it. On a commissioned piece you have to check yourself—be careful to do what the client wants." [59]

The results of these experiments and observations of Deming, Deci, Herzberg, and Csikszentmihalyi all lead us towards one conclusion: the current structure behind work, jobs, work as obligation, of trading time doing an undesirable task, a disutility isn't just undesirable, it's also ineffective for doing great work.

MO' MEANING MO' MONEY

In an interview, Joel Spolsky, founder of Stack Overflow, a question and answer site for computer programming related questions that advertises job opportunities to programmers, discussed his experience having seen thousands of computer programmers hired through his site.[60]

In order to get a developer to go to Goldman Sachs, you would typically have to pay them at least double what it might take to get him to go to a company where he finds the work meaningful.

It's also unlikely he'd do anything useful. When's the last time something innovative came out of Goldman Sachs?

As a society, we're paying people more money to do things which create less wealth. Yet we're at a point where we can create more wealth and make more money for ourselves and others by pursuing work which forces us to grow in a way we personally find meaningful.

Work has always been a disutility because the work that was required to accumulate more wealth and address the economic limit was primarily simple, algorithmic or at best, complicated work. If you're a farmer and you were trying to get a job in the city one hundred years ago, you were probably going to end up in a factory. That was the opportunity available. The barriers to starting your own business were far higher than they are today.

Marc Andreessen recounted in an interview how the first meeting he has with entrepreneurs that approach him about backing their company usually plays out. They always reach a point, fairly early on in the interview, where Marc will start trying to talk the founders out of the idea and suggesting other ways to attack the problem than the one they've outlined or proposing a different problem to attack. That moment in the conversation has proved to be the biggest predictor of success with companies that Andreessen Horowitz funds.

Successful founders he meets have tried every other reasonable plan of attack on the problem, and it is the most important problem they can imagine. When Andreesen starts suggesting other ways to attack it, founders doomed for failure tend to turn into "yes men" and are suddenly ready to change gears. The most successful founders start getting angry and either walk out or threaten to walk out. They've spent thousands of hours thinking about and working on the problem. Having someone that's barely considered it for fifteen minutes start suggesting other problems to attack or ways to attack it only pisses them off.

When Yahoo attempted to acquire Facebook for $1 billion in 2006, Zuckerberg met with his two primary investors, Peter Thiel and Jim Breyer.

Breyer and Thiel believed they should sell, but Zuckerberg started the meeting with an offhand remark: "This is kind of a formality, just a quick board meeting, it shouldn't take more than 10 minutes. We're obviously not going to sell here."

Had they taken the deal, Zuckerberg would have cashed out for $250 million, but in Zuckerberg's mind, the only thing he would do with the money was start another social networking site. He liked the one he already had and found working on it meaningful.

As of 2015, Facebook's market capitalization is $230 billion. Thiel and Breyer are both happy to have lost that argument and let Zuckerberg keep working on Facebook.[61]

Adam Grant, a psychologist from the University of Pennsylvania, found the same phenomenon in an experiment at a call center. He divided up call center representatives into three separate groups. All three groups were making calls for a university fundraising operation. The first group was instructed to read about the personal benefits of the job, such as making money and developing communication skills. The second group read stories about people who had received scholarships from the money raised and how it had improved their lives before hitting the phones . The third group served as the control. The control group and first group instructed to read up on the benefits performed the same.

However, the second group, the group that understood the purpose behind their work, raised twice as much money.[62]

The biggest problem we're dealing with today is the underutilization of individuals. The most talented and ambitious young people, when they feel under-utilized in the jobs, shrink to fit their position.

Complex entrepreneurial work is what is in short supply, and jobs where we are working as an obligation hurt our ability to do that. It's hurting us as a society, but more importantly it's hurting us as individuals. If we're seeking to do our best work and to create a legacy, it's not taking us there.

For the first time in history, we've reached a point where humans' natural drive to strive and grow by working on interesting problems aligns with what the market demands. It's not only in congruence with fundamental human drives—it's more economically valuable. Finding meaning in your work isn't just fulfilling. It's a profitable business strategy.

FRANKL AND THE EMERGENCE OF THE EXISTENTIAL VACUUM

Viktor Frankl, a psychologist raised in Austria in the 1920's, was given a chance before Hitler invaded Austria to escape to America, but he opted to stay with his family in Austria. When the Nazis arrived, he and his family were promptly rounded up and deported to a concentration camp.

Over the course of the war, Frankl's entire family was murdered. Frankl himself survived half a decade in the most abject, horrific environment imaginable, moving between a trio of camps including the infamous Auschwitz.

In his time in the concentration camps, Frankl observed that traditional theories of motivation and survival didn't explain why some prisoners lived and others died. All prisoners were subject to the same inhumane conditions of depersonalization, violent abuse, and overwork. They were all undernourished and over-worked beyond human comprehension.

Why did some prisoners struggle to survive where others died?

He saw the same scenario play out over and over. When a prisoner found out his family had died, they often quickly followed. For prisoners that defined their family as what gave them meaning, it was impossible to endure the hell of a concentration camp knowing their families wouldn't be there to greet them on the other side.

His observations lead Frankl to develop the theory of logotherapy in his book, *Man's Search for Meaning*. Unlike previous theories of motivation, like Freud's Will to Pleasure or Nietzsche's Will to Power, Frankl saw that the fundamental thing people sought was meaning. There was no power or pleasure to be had in a concentration camp. There was, however, a way to find meaning.

WHOOSH GOES THE EXISTENTIAL VACUUM

Despite access to a higher quality and quantity of consumer items than ever, Frankl observed an increasing level of discontent among his patients. This existential vacuum, or lack of meaning, has become a widespread phenomenon in the West during the 20th century. Existentialism as a school of philosophical thought has shaped much of Western thinking.

But where did it come from?

The seeds of this discontent and unhappiness were planted early in the history of humanity, just a few miles past the fork away from our more ape-like relatives. The development of the frontal lobe in humans means that, unlike apes, humans are not driven wholly by instinct. We evolved the ability to process and make decisions.

This is no trivial or marginal change. It's that ability to make decisions that have led to our dominance on Earth. Unlike any other species, we must make choices.

For most of human history, this didn't create too many issues. There weren't a tremendous number of choices to be made, and for those that did exist, larger institutions dictated to the mass of people the traditions they abided by.

From tribal leaders to governments to corporations, the structure of our society was set up for us. If you live in a tribe of hunter gatherers, or in a small town with a local church and a manufacturing plant, you didn't have a tremendous number of choices, and those you did have were driven by those institutions. The tribesman hunts when the hunting party goes out and celebrates the winter solstice on the shortest day of the year. The small town resident goes to church on Sundays, works during the week, and goes to company functions on Saturdays.

Let's do a quick catch up before moving on:

- We're goal-seeking, striving creatures.
- We seek goals which create meaning and freedom in our lives.
- The lack of meaning is a modern problem.

- It's solved by pursuing a goal greater than ourselves.

- In doing so, we actually produce more valuable work, are happier, and as a side effect, make more money.

Tradition has continued to erode even more than when Frankl wrote his book, making it more difficult to figure out what that goal is both for us individually and for us as a society. As tradition continues to dissolve, the existential vacuum is ever more present.

We, more than any other generation before us, must truly *choose* how to structure our lives. Compared with our parents, we have far less tradition and structure in our lives. Yet at the same time, we have far more opportunity. A great blessing to be sure, but it forces us to decide, to ask: What do we want?

For most, this leads to one of two outcomes:

1. A desire to do what other people do: conformity.

2. Doing what other people tell them to do: totalitarianism.

A THIRD WAY AND THE HALLWAY TEST

For the Baby Boomer generation, there was a relatively clearly-defined generational promise. The GI Bill and the unprecedented economic opportunity that emerged in the Post WWII era gave them something to grow into. They had to do the work to step into it, but it was pretty clear what the opportunity was.

For most of our generation, there isn't a clearly-defined opportunity or generational promise.

I recently spoke with Tom. Tom is in his mid-thirties and does a bunch of odd contract jobs and hustles to make money selling things on eBay then goes out and enjoys life, parties, travels, and has fun.

Ten years ago, when he graduated from college, he set out on a career to be a high school teacher. He loved teaching and loved working with kids. About five years in, he was frustrated with the system. He was teaching students things he didn't believe were helpful or meaningful to him or them, but it was what the schooling system's standardized test required.

One summer, visiting with a group of his friends that were SCUBA diving instructors, he expressed his frustration. When they continued to probe him, he realized that not only was he unhappy with the work, but at the end of the year, his "good job" compared to his friends freelancing as Scuba instructors led to the same amount of money saved up: Zero.

Why would he give up all his time teaching in a school that forced him to deliver a curriculum he didn't believe in and end up with a zero in the bank account?

Linda, a woman in her late 60s, was in a similar situation early on in her career. She worked as a teacher for a while and used that job to help her husband survive and pay for law school. Eventually she became his office manager and they worked together and built something ambitious and meaningful. A law practice that created a level of freedom out of reach of their parents who had grown up on a rural farm.

Unlike our parents' generation, there isn't a lot of upward trajectory in that path anymore. More student debt and stagnating wages would mean a larger debt to pay off for her and her husband, and less income to pay it off with.

Even if a couple did manage to replicate it, it would, for many, feel dramatically less fulfilling. It wouldn't be much of a stretch. It would be working very hard to end up somewhere that wasn't compelling or inspiring to be in the first place.

If you're in a job that forces you to do something you don't want to be doing and doesn't have much upward trajectory, you might as well quit your job teaching and go be a SCUBA instructor. If you don't have something to reach for and strive, you may as well just chill out.

Many people in traditional, corporate jobs face a similar situation. They have the same desire to grow and create value for others and strive for something meaningful. Corporate management likes to use buzzwords like "networking" and "getting exposure," but it always feels rather insignificant.

Doubt always lingers. Is this helping myself and what I want? Is this really helping anyone at all?

If you look at someone five years ahead of you professionally, like looking down the hallway at an office, is that someone whose life you want?

When you perform the look-down-the-hallway test to see what the people in their company five years ahead of you are doing, are you excited about that future?

MORE THAN YOU EVER IMAGINED POSSIBLE

Frankl realized in the concentration camp that his purpose and what gave his life meaning was to reveal his theory on the will to meaning, logotherapy, to the world. It was that goal that kept him alive through five years in hell. Instead of smuggling food, he would smuggle around small pieces of paper on which he would write out his evolving theory.

Fortunately, Frankly identified other ways than surviving a concentration camp to discover meaning. The primary method he cites is that of creating a work or doing a deed. It is something to be discovered by going out into the world and creating, not within our own psyche. What that act is for each individual is different.

The opportunity for our generation is that the tools to do the deed, to generate the work, to go out into the world and create, have never been more accessible, safer.

For the first time in human history, the pursuit of money,

meaning, and freedom through entrepreneurship are more profitable and synergistic than ever before.

CONCLUSION

The Future of Work

MANY PEOPLE I TALKED TO IN THE PROCESS OF WRITING this asked me, do you really think that's happening?

You really think that we're moving into this amazing period of freedom and wealth as entrepreneurs?

The short answer: maybe.

I don't believe this is a future that will create itself. The opportunity is real. I've seen and talked with hundreds of people that have grabbed it. But, it's one of many possible futures.

Another future is a return to a pre-20th century paradigm, outlined by forecasters like French economist Thomas Piketty. Piketty's premise is that before the 20th century, the rate of return on capital almost always exceeded the rate of economic growth; wealth grows faster than the economy; the rich get richer and the poor get poorer.

Data exists to back him up. While the rate of return on capital for the average adult has been 2.1% since 1987, it's been 6.5% for the average billionaire.

Yet, there are two ways of looking at this. The first is continuing with Piketty's view: the rich are going to get richer and we're doomed to live in an unequal society.

The other is that Piketty's view is short-sighted and historical facing. That those same tools, the means of production, available exclusively to the wealthy for all of human history, are now in your hands. Multimillion-dollar businesses are run using a laptop, Skype, and an internet connection. That is the world in which we live. One where the future is not defined. One where it's up to each individual, group, and society to write the future for themselves.

What Piketty and others like him fail to see is that never before has a generation held the pen to write their future in the way we do—but it will not write itself.

BECOMING DEFINITE OPTIMISTS

We live in a society defined by what venture capitalist Peter Thiel calls indefinite optimism. While we all sense on some level the expanding amount of possibility and opportunity available to us, you must step up to seize it. While many feel destined for something more, something bigger, few of us have taken actions to seize it. We are optimistic, but unwilling to define for ourselves what that optimism looks like.

"The project can wait."

"I'm sure it will work out fine."

The Baby Boomer generation, unlike our generation, was firmly definite in their optimism. The wealth they created was not something they hoped would happen, but one which they seized. The moments which stand out in their lives are those of bold pronouncements and plans to realize them.

In 1962, President Kennedy defined the future of space exploration and a country rallied behind him. "We choose to go to the moon in this decade and do the other things, not because they are easy, but because they are hard." [63]

President Reagan defined the future of a unified Germany: "Mr. Gorbachev, tear down this wall."

Martin Luther King had a dream and marched on the nation's capital to make it a reality.

We have abdicated this responsibility.

Thiel sees this in the proliferation of "wealth re-arrangers" in today's society. Massive industries, from law to finance, are dedicated not to creating more wealth but to simply moving money around in a circle. While we believe everything will improve (otherwise we wouldn't invest) it's unclear how. Diversification reigns supreme.

When a successful individual invests, they give their money to a large bank. The bankers don't know what to do with it, so they diversify it across a portfolio of institutional investors. The institutional investors, equally clueless, spread it out across a portfolio of stocks. Those companies then try to increase their share price and, if they succeed, issue dividends or buyback shares, and the whole cycle repeats.[64]

No one actually knows what to do with the money to create more wealth.

Given the amount of capital, opportunity, and possibility available to us today, we still aren't investing in a definite future. We feel it, but we're just sort of hopeful.

You know who thinks like that?

A nation that has been trained to believe in work as an obligation, in the traditional job paradigm. A nation that looks at jobs reports as a measure of productivity. We generally believe that things will get better and that the company will grow *because* we have a very minimal amount of control over it.

Because entrepreneurship has historically been more difficult to invest in and jobs have had better returns, this was a belief that never got us into much trouble. We accepted the lack of control and it worked out.

That's no longer a good trade off.

The structure of our world has been transformed. We live in Extremistan, a world defined by its unpredictability and rapid change. Advances in communication technology and global education standards are pulling pre-industrial economies into the industrial economy creating a motivated, global workforce to compete with.

Someone whose grandparents grew up on a farm in Vietnam without electricity is now highly educated, motivated and connected to the global marketplace. At the same time, machines in the West are replacing many of the repetitive tasks that occupied a great deal of humanity in an Industrial, factory-based economy.

We've reached the end of jobs. The implicit promise of jobs made to our parents of long-term, stable employment is dying. We've over invested in traditional credentials at a time when many jobs are being moved overseas or replaced by machines.

Yet, a certain group, entrepreneurs, are beset, overwhelmed by opportunity. While these changes make it more competitive and less profitable than ever to find a job where you can take orders and rest safely at night knowing nothing dramatic is about to happen, they make it possible for the first time to seize a level of wealth, freedom, and meaning without precedent in human history.

WHO ARE YOU?

What are the first words that popped to mind? Son? Brother? American? Employee?

When asked to define ourselves, we rarely truly do so. We instead define ourselves by the institutions that define us. Son and brother to our family. American to our nation. Employee to our company.

Entrepreneur is unlike any of these. It is categorically different. Entrepreneur to whom exactly?

While the expansion in freedom and wealth that's taken place over the last few centuries is remarkable, it pales in comparison to what we're going through right now.

Democracy expanded the power to choose our leader. Corporations expanded our power to choose our employers.

Entrepreneurship expands your power to design your life. You are a part of the first generation that has radical access to the tools of production. Rather than choosing from a set of options, you can design your own.

The internet and technology have revealed the power of the Long Tail. As major markets fragment into smaller and smaller markets, there's more opportunities. The democratization of production and distribution means it's easier than ever to take advantage of them and design your own reality.

Social scripts like stair stepping and apprenticeships make it possible to invest in entrepreneurship and become more entrepreneurial have been created that didn't exist a decade ago.

In Extremistan, they've paved the way to investing in something that's not only more accessible, but also safer. As work becomes increasingly complex, only those that adapt to the new paradigm are secure in any meaningful sense.

The limit we're at as a society for economic and structural reasons lines up with our fundamental human drives for more money, more meaning, and more freedom.

WHAT WILL BE YOUR LEGACY?

> *"Washington is not a place to live in. The rents are high, the food is bad, the dust is disgusting and the morals are deplorable. Go West, young man, go West and grow up with the country."*
>
> – HORACE GREELEY TO THE SETTLERS OF THE AMERICAN WEST IN THE 1800S

After graduating college, Rob Walling was a project manager at a construction company where his dad had worked for over 42 years. He knew all the founders and was quickly put in a management track heading for the corner office.

He quit just over ten years ago when he had a gut feeling that he was "slated for something different or something bigger."

> *"It's interesting that I say bigger because I run a company that's way, way, way smaller than the company that I was potentially going to become an executive at, but felt like in my gut, I was 22 years old at the time, that if I looked back on my life at 65 and I had worked for this electrical contractor my whole life, even as an executive, am I going to be happy? What's my legacy? Am I going to be happy with that legacy? And the answer was no. I wanted to do something that was more interesting to me. And that was technology, and that was building software which lead to writing books and blogs and podcasting. I had no idea all that was going to happen, but now that it is, I've realized that this is where I should be. I'm ten times happier doing what I am now than if I had stayed the course."*

> *"The legacy part for me is that as it stands now, I have impacted so many more people than I ever could have because I now have a blog and a podcast and a conference and the talks that I do. And that, to me, is my legacy. That is what I think will outlast. There wouldn't have been the impact of really helping people had I stayed the course."* [65]

If you look back at what you got accomplished in the last week, it probably feels like you didn't do nearly enough. If you look back at what you've accomplished in the last three years, it probably feels a lot more substantial. Maybe you finished a big project or learned a new language or made a host of new, meaningful relationships.

We tend to overestimate our ability to get things done in the short term, but underestimate our ability to get things done in the long term.

It feels really important to answer all my emails right now; someone is waiting on it! It feels important to read all those Buzzfeed articles popping up on Facebook.

But what if, instead of answering the email or reading those articles, you spent an hour every day working on that project you've been thinking about? Writing a book; launching a product on the side to begin stair stepping; looking for an apprenticeship with a company you admire; building a business that you could tell your grandchildren about.

If you were to look back in three years, do you think it would be more important to have answered the email or worked on that project?

Framed like that, it's pretty obvious. If I look at the goals I set for myself three years ago, where I imagined I would be, I massively underestimated myself. Almost everyone I know does the same.

Now extend that out over a lifetime. If we underestimate what we can accomplish in three years, how much are we underestimating ourselves over the next thirty years?

Each generation, each person, has some latent potential inside of them. An opportunity to be realized. Our great grandparents settled the American West. Our grandparents stormed the beaches of Normandy and saved a continent from Nazism and fascism. Our parents created an unprecedented level of wealth in the *Pax Americana* era that followed.

We do not have the luxuries of their generations. No president will call you up to your destiny as they may have your great-grandparents or grandparents; no CEO will lay out the path for you. Fifty years from now, as you look back on your life, the story you have to tell will have been one you alone have written.

Never before in human history has an individual staring at his world had a greater ability to craft that story into one that now exists only in your imagination. You have the opportunity, right now, to design the future. Your future. Our future. To write a story where you have more control over your reality, more freedom, more money, and more meaning that anyone alive a century ago could have imagined.

The blank screen, the blinking cursor. Write, young man, write.

To get access to all the free resources included with the book (listed below), please visit **http://taylorpearson.me/eoj**

- Full Recorded Interviews with the ten entrepreneurs featured in *The End of Jobs,* detailing how they launched their own successful businesses.

- 67 Business Books to Fuel Your Entrepreneurial Career.

- 49 Tools and Templates to use when launching and growing a business.

- A ninety-day goal setting worksheet to translate the book into actionable steps, and move you towards building an entrepreneurial career of freedom, meaning, and wealth.

- Access to a private community to discuss the book, and get support from a community of like-minded individuals.

NEXT STEPS

Why Successful People Plan Their Lives 90 Days at a Time (Template Included)

In *Mastering the Rockefeller Habits,* Verne Harnish advocates planning on a ninety-day time frame.

I remember thinking: "That seems a little extreme, Verne. Really, you only plan 90 days?"

There is a large class of activities, however, for which the "middle" route is the worst place to fall.

Research shows that when you exercise, you want to either go for long rambling walks or do quick intense workouts. It's the long, moderate amounts of activity that get people in trouble.[66]

When you live in a city, you want to live in the middle of

the action downtown, or way out in the country where it's calm and relaxing. You *don't* want to get caught in suburban purgatory.

If you're giving a presentation, either move fast and keep it tactical like "my five step process for going viral on Facebook," or keep it broad and inspirational—"why today is the best day ever to market on Facebook." The worst talks are always ones where they fall in the middle. "We do a lot of social media marketing. Facebook is the best for social media marketing." Wow, thanks for that. For what kind of business? How often do you post? What do you post about? What size image do you use? Those would be helpful things to know.

Physical items you own, like clothes and bags, are a middle-way-is-the-worst-way phenomenon as well. You typically either want really nice stuff you'll keep for years or really cheap stuff you won't mind throwing away.

Gary Vaynerchuk of VaynerMedia and Wine Library TV has identified the same phenomenon, calling it the Clouds and the Dirt. He's either thinking in the day-to-day minutia of exactly how to post on Facebook—how many words should the post be?—or how to buy the New York Jets (where is marketing going over the next decade? How are we positioned for it?).

Reading through venture capitalist Marc Andreessen's Guide to Career Planning, I was pleasantly unsurprised by his number one piece of advice on the topic:

Don't.

The first rule of career planning: Do not plan your career.

The world is an incredibly complex place and everything is changing all the time. You can't plan your career because you have no idea what's going to happen in the future... Trying to plan your career is an exercise in futility that will only serve to frustrate you, and to blind you to the really significant opportunities that life will throw your way.

...

The second rule of career planning: Instead of planning your career, focus on developing skills and pursuing opportunities.[67]

Times change—when we're talking in years, it changes five to ten times faster than you think.

Researcher Roy Amara noted this in his formulation of what's come to be called Amara's Law:

We tend to overestimate the effect of a technology in the short run and underestimate the effect in the long run.

The same is true of ourselves. We dramatically underestimate how much we can get done in two or three years, but *overestimate* how much we can get done in a day or a week.

SUCCESSFUL PEOPLE PLAN 90 DAYS AT A TIME

From my experience and from entrepreneurs I've worked with,

Verne Harnish was about spot on for planning: Ninety days seems to be the range where ambition and planning actually fall reasonably close together.

Looking ninety days out, you have a good idea of what you can actually get done in that time frame. Your capacity estimations are about right, and yet you can make some very substantial progress towards a big goal.

It leads to moving faster without compromising strategy. Having goals and visions for three to five years down the line is valuable in terms of knowing which direction you want to move, but it's often not very helpful to try and plan out concrete steps—there's just too much that has to get done, which feels overwhelming and leads to inaction.

However, you probably have a pretty good idea of what opportunities are on your plate right now and how you can capitalize on them in the next ninety days.

Maybe you know of a business you could approach about an apprenticeship. Or you have an idea for a small product to get you started. Or you know you want to learn copywriting.

Once you launch those projects, new opportunities will pop up, and you can look at those in ninety days and reassess whether they're heading in the right direction or not.

Below, I've included the template I went through leading up to the release of this book as an example. Read through it and then go to **http://taylorpearson.me/eoj/** to download a copy of the template yourself.

90 DAY PLANNING TEMPLATE

Review and Update Your "Perfect Day." If you could do anything without chance of failure, what would you do? What would a perfect day look like? What would make you most excited to wake up and do tomorrow? Write this like it were a movie script of your life.

It's not very helpful to "plan"—break things down into action steps—on a longer time frame, but keeping the destination or direction in mind when I review and plan helps to manage your motivation and goals more effectively. I can see how everything I do on a day-to-day basis is taking me towards where I want to go or if they aren't taking me there, stop doing them! Write out this document as though it were a movie script of your life. What would you have for breakfast? What time would you do each action?

Quarterly Review

The purpose of the review is to force yourself to re-orient and most importantly "get real" with the way things are moving. Denial is not just a river in Egypt, it's also a good a way to avoid doing the work that matters.

1. **Define the Key Role** (*If you name the role well, that's almost*

half the work; try to get as detailed and specific as possible. What would someone call the role you're trying to live?)

   a. I am an entrepreneur and author.

2. **What would I do in the next twelve weeks if I had no momentum and couldn't fail?** (i.e. *If you could start from scratch, what would you do? Momentum matters, but only if it's moving you in the right direction. To quote Peter Drucker, "There is nothing so useless as doing efficiently that which should not be done at all."*)

   a. I would write an Amazon bestselling book about entrepreneurship as a platform builder.

3. **Take stock—Where am I**? (*This is where you can start to incorporate momentum as well, what assets you have as figuring out where you need to course correct and what just needs to get flat out dropped.*)

   a. What went well? What were three things I did right and should do more of?

      i. Writing consistently.

      ii. Shipping the writing earlier than felt comfortable to alpha and beta readers.

   b. What went badly? What were the biggest mistakes I made? Why didn't I achieve what I set out to achieve?

   i. I don't have a final draft of the book done, about two weeks behind schedule.

   ii. I'm off pace in terms of growing my website in terms of email subscribers.

c. What are the three least valuable things I'm doing? What am I doing to avoid the truly important work?

   i. Everything not dramatically increasing traffic and conversions in terms of tinkering with the site.

   ii. Writing more than twice a month on my own site is useless without the marketing to support it; better to focus on other platforms with more momentum.

   iii. I still don't have as clearly defined of a brand promise as I'd like for people to rally behind, writing and brand promise is all over the place.

4. **The Goal: Where do I want to be twelve weeks from now? If I am reading this twelve weeks from today, what has to have happened for me to feel happy with my progress?** (*Here I'm trying to figure out what the right level of ambition for a goal is. Because ninety days seems to be the sweet spot in terms of estimating ambition and capacity, this is usually something that feels challenging, yet achievable. Once I figure out what that is, I define criteria around it that will hold me accountable.*)

a. Where do I *really* want to be in twelve weeks, but I'm too embarrassed to say it out loud?

    i. Twelve weeks from now, I want to have a bestselling book launched on Amazon.

b. Clearly Define a Goal and KPIs Maximum of three KPIs for each role, though one is best. These must be either a clearly defined, falsifiable result (e.g. Published a book, have 5,000 email subscribers)

    i. Publish a Book on Amazon

    ii. Double Email List Size

5. **The Why—Why do I want to be there? What's the importance?** (*The goal isn't important—it's* what *it lets you do. The "why" is also what gets you to emotionally commit, so it has to be big, vibrant, and clear. I try to be completely honest with myself. If it's a vanity-based thing that gets me excited, I'll say that. Going through the "why" section will typically force me to go up and edit the goal if they don't feel properly aligned. I have to go back and make darn sure it's justified given I'm planning on spending a chunk of my life working on it.*)

    a. I think we're at a unique moment in human history where power is dispersing from organizations to individuals. I believe that the opportunity in technology (mainly that the internet has brought) is that it has distributed power to the individuals in a way no one ever imagined was possible, and once people realize that and see how to seize it, we can realize the entrepreneurial economy. I think the book can help push that forward. I want to create freedom and opportunity for myself to invest more in my writing. I want to shape a generational conversation around entrepreneurship and be respected as a thought leader. I want to launch a product and better understand running a product as opposed to a consulting business.

6. **The How—How do I get there?** (*This is where I'm bridging the gap and starting to get into what the details that really need to get taken care of are.*)

    a. What dangers do you have now that need to be eliminated?

        i. The biggest dangers I have that I need to eliminate are creating things that are not value innovation. Technological or idea innovation are valuable only when it can be translated into value innovation. Some of the writing is overly philosophical and unhelpful when it needs to be more prescriptive and actionable.

        ii. The other big danger I see myself falling into is over focusing on product and under focusing on marketing distribution. Until the platform gets substantially larger, I need to be spending at least as much effort on distribution and outreach to larger platforms as I am to my own platform.

b. What opportunities need to be captured?

   i. The biggest opportunities I see that need to be captured are guest posting, podcasting interviews, and syndication through more established platforms. Basically: more marketing and outreach.

   ii. I think there's also a very real opportunity to position and market the book in such a way as to draft off of larger, more established platforms that share the vision/mission of the book, and then turning that expanded field into more outreach, speaking, consulting in line with the book vision.

c. What strengths need to be maximized?

   i. The biggest strengths I have that need to be maximized are my existing network and personal connections as well as SOPs and other systems I have built out internally that I can use to add value.

d. What does the day-to-day life of someone that has already achieved this goal look like?

   i. On an average day, someone that has achieved this goal prioritizes marketing and outreach and distribution over product, and "done" over "good." They don't overthink; they focus on doing the work that matters, not busy work and shipping early and often. They prioritize the emotional work and let the rest fall off the edges.

(Reminder: *I've included a download for all these templates at* **http://taylorpearson.me/eoj**

Q2 Big Initiatives

Once I've gone through and done the review, I break it out into a document (usually in Evernote) that I can reference throughout the quarter for monthly and weekly planning to carry the "review" content into action steps.

Become a Best-Selling Author (copied from Question 1 of the review)

1. Why (*copied from question 5 of the review*): I think we're at a unique moment in human history where power is dispersing from organizations to individuals. I believe that the opportunity in technology (mainly that the internet has brought) is that it has distributed power to the individuals in a way no one ever imagined was possible, and once people realize that and see how to seize it, we can realize the entrepreneurial economy. I think the book can help push that forward. I want to create freedom and opportunity for myself to invest more in my writing. I want to shape a generational conversation around entrepreneurship and be respected as a thought leader. I want to launch a product and better understand running a product as opposed to a consulting business.

2. How (*copied from question 6 and converted into phrases that start action verbs*):

a. Launch new opt-in

    i. Introduction

    ii. Toolkit

b. Review and update draft of book based on exclusive early reader feedback

c. Execute book marketing

    i. Reach out to people in network with book marketing experience to finalize marketing plan

    ii. Aggressively schedule guest posts and podcast interview

d. Actively prioritize "done" over "good" and distribution over product

3. Result/KPIs (*copied from question 4 and something I look at daily*):

    a. Books Sold/Product Revenue

    b. Email Subscribers

April Big Initiatives

Now that you've got the quarter roughly planned out, take the major quarterly goals and break them down into smaller action steps for the next month.

Send Final Content to Editor

1. Why (*copied again from the review*): I think we're at a unique moment in human history where power is dispersing from organizations to individuals. I believe that the opportunity in technology (mainly that the internet has brought) is that it has distributed power to the individuals in a way no one ever imagined was possible, and once people realize that and see how to seize it, we can realize the entrepreneurial economy. I think the book can help push that forward. I want to create freedom and opportunity for myself to invest more in my writing. I want to shape a generational conversation around entrepreneurship and be respected as a thought leader. I want to launch a product and better understand running a product as opposed to a consulting business.

2. How (*What actions would make everything else easier or unnecessary? What actions need to get done first?*):

    a. Publish and promote two blog posts.

    b. Get pre-launch group into a Facebook group and set-up a plan to consistently add value to group.

    c. Line up guest posts and podcast interviews for launch in June.

d. Put together opt-ins/giveaways on website.

e. Get research interviews edited and uploaded to libsyn to launch as a podcast.

f. Launch new opt-in with book intro and tools.

g. Review early reader feedback and map out next draft vision and hit list for editing

h. Final content revision.

3. Result/KPI:

a. Final content revision sent to editor.

b. Twenty confirmed podcast/guest posts for launch period.

c. Intro/toolkit opt-in launched.

Weekly Planning

Now, repeat the exact same process for the monthly goals and break them down into weekly.

Finish final content edit of Section 1 and 2 of *The End of Jobs* Manuscript

1. Why (*copied again from the review*): I think we're at a unique moment in human history where power is dispersing from organizations to individuals. I believe that the opportunity in technology (mainly that the internet has brought) is that it has distributed power to the individuals in a way no one ever imagined was possible, and once people realize that and see how to seize it, we can realize the entrepreneurial economy. I think the book can help push that forward. I want to create freedom and opportunity for myself to invest more in my writing. I want to shape a generational conversation around entrepreneurship and be respected as a thought leader. I want to launch a product and better understand running a product as opposed to a consulting business.

2. How: (*Try and sort them into two- to three-hour chunks and assign two to three to each day since that's realistically how much work you're going to do over the course of the week.*)

    a. Monday

        i. Revise Section 1 according to early reader feedback synthesis.

        ii. Define User flow for marketing on site and for opt-ins post-launch.

        iii. Team meeting and management.

    b. Tuesday

    i. Revise Section 2 Part 1 according to Early Reader Feedback Synthesis.

    ii. Document.

    iii. Talk to Tom and finalize book marketing.

    iv. Consulting/coaching.

c. Wednesday

    i. Draft planning system article and send to Kimberly to edit.

    ii. Send podcast episodes and updated SOP to podcast editor.

    iii. Consulting/coaching.

d. Thursday

    i. Revise planning system post and send to Marissa to upload.

    ii. Consulting/coaching.

e. Friday

    i. Revise Section 2 Part 2 according to Early Reader Feedback Synthesis document.

    ii. Finalize article for this week.

    iii. Do something to add value in Facebook group.

3. Results/KPIs (*These are the definitive tasks to have done at the end of the week to judge by*):

    a. Finished Content Edit of Section 1 and 2 sent to editors.

    b. Send Podcasts to Editor.

    c. Define/Finalize Marketing Plan and week by week timelines.

    d. Next Steps with Consulting Work.

Daily Planning

Morning

Instructions:

Do this in a physical notebook at the start of the morning after looking at your weekly list.

I am Grateful For...(list a **minimum** of three things, *nothing motivates more than gratitude*)

1. Better understanding my own psychology

2. The opportunities in Austin

3. The book my Dad sent me

What Would Make Today Great is (List **maximum** of three things that push forward weekly Objectives)

1. Send article to editor

2. Review edits for sections 1 and 2 of book

3. Finalize book marketing timeline

I am a great...(List *minimum* of three affirmations)

1. Entrepreneur

2. Author

3. Strength Athlete

A CRITICAL, FINAL STEP

The critical final step is to put these in a place where you will look over them every single day. Far too many goal setting exercises leave people feeling great after they set goals, but don't force them to confront those goals and make the hard decisions required to achieve them on a day-to-day basis.

I personally like to put them in an Evernote note and save them to the shortcuts of my Evernote for daily review.

You can also print them out, but make sure to incorporate them into a morning ritual to review on a daily basis.

To download a free copy of all my templates, including this 90 Day Goal Setting Action Step Template, go to http://taylorpearson.me/eoj and enter your email.

P.S. Many smart people have read this book but I'm sure we missed things. If you notice any corrections, send them to Corrections@TaylorPearson.Me*—I'd very much appreciate it! Thank you!*

ACKNOWLEDGEMENTS

I WANT TO DEEPLY THANK THE EARLY READERS WHO GAVE feedback on articles related to the book and volunteered to read portions of the early manuscript: Mark Manson, Jodi Ettenberg, Steven Moody, Bret Funk, Hudson Baird, Bruce Berger, Diego Sueiro, Bruce Berger, Glen Thompson, Paulo Ribeiro, Brent Passmore, Steffen Krogmann, Roberto Zoia, Ian Obrien, Brian Guanzon, Marcos Haftel, Jeff Doehler, Nirvana Cable, Juan Ramon Anton, Joshua Skaja, Chiara Cokieng, Cory Ames, Jeff Pecaro, Jimmy Tomczak, Derek Szeto, Marcos Haftel, Ben Gelsey, Octavio Urzua, Billy Breuer, Joanna Rives, Bryce Ferguson, Bruno Cavalcanti, Derek Dodds, Taylor Letterman, Richard Pearson, Kris Jones, Laura Hanly, Betty Jean Bell, Ryan Kaufman, Jeff Pawlak, Steve Reck, Yishi Zuo, Nathan Tsang, Kendra Kinnison, Rainer Groh, Will Boucek, Will Ward, Dan Trzil, Ragnar Ranøyen Homb, Stan Leloup, Vishnu Narayanan, Mirko S., Alex Thornton, Stephan Iscoe, Jason Brunson, Vlad Stan, Max Mackey, George Millo, Mike

Cautillo, Evan Webb, Alex Kozack, Tom Gole, Johnny Curran, Mike Dariano, Jonathan Strong, Heather Chauhan, Alex Cantrill, Dan Volgenau and Louie Dinh.

I suspect less than 10% of the original version made it into the final version and the iterations in between were very much due to your feedback.

I have a special debt of gratitude to those who read VERY early versions and multiple versions: Dan Andrews, George Millo, Laura Hanly, Will Boucek, David Hilgeman, Casey Ames, Mike Eads, Mike Stankavich, Jason Brunson, Ragnar Ranøyen Homb, Steven Moody, Kendra Kinnison, Cory Ames, Casey Ames, Ben Gelsey, Mike Dariano, Marissa Semilla, and Rainer Groh.

Thank you to Mike Covel, who pushed me over the edge to write the book.

Thank you to the editing team from Craft Your Content—Elisa Doucette, Kimberly Martin, Sherise Van Dyk, and Melody Boggs. You can contact them about editing services at **CraftYourContent.com**

To Dan Andrews and Ian Schoen: thanks for the apprenticeship. It changed everything for me.

Thank you to the Masterminds I've been a part of over the past two years who have pushed me forward and made this book a reality through support and stories.

Thanks to all the writers who have inspired me over the years:

Seth Godin, James Altucher, Verne Harnish, Ron Davison, Nassim Taleb, Peter Drucker, Steven Pressfield, Venkatesh Rao, Dan Andrews, Mark Manson, Jodi Ettenberg, to name just a few.

Thank you to everyone that helped get the book out and allowed me the opportunity to speak about it. Tom Morkes of Insurgent Publishing and **TomMorkes.com**, Christopher Sherrod of **christophersherrod.com**, and Chandler Bolt of Self-Publishing School. Thank you to Derek Murphy of **creativindie.com** for his help with the cover design. Thank you to the team **bookinabox.com** for their help with the formatting and layout design.

Thank you to the entrepreneurs who were generous enough with their time to share their stories. The hundreds of you that did so informally, and also Dan Andrews, Rob Walling, Dan Norris, Andrew Youderian, Derek Sivers, Perry Marshall, John McIntyre, Elisa Doucette, Jesse Lawler, and Billy Murphy who did so formally and whose interviews you can download at **http://taylorpearson.me/eoj**

To Mom, Dad, Inge, Heather, Ravi, Reid and Claire: Thanks and Love. :)

Last, but certainly not least, thank you to all the members of the Dynamite Circle community without whose support this book would not be possible.

NOTES

SECTION 1

1. http://www.nytimes.com/2009/03/13/business/economy/13wealth.html?_r=0
2. Steve Jobs - https://www.youtube.com/watch?v=UvEiSa6_EPA
3. Source: http://www.kpcb.com/internet-trends, 2015 report, slides 97-98
4. http://www.nytimes.com/2013/02/20/business/college-degree-required-by-increasing-number-of-companies.html?ref=business&_r=1&

CHAPTER 1

5. http://www.chrisducker.com/how-much-do-i-pay-my-virtual-assistant/
6. http://dazeinfo.com/2014/10/28/1-5-million-engineering-pass-outs-india-every-year-fewer-getting-hired-trends/
7. http://www.engineeringuk.com/View/?con_id=360
8. http://www.oecd.org/edu/50495363.pdf
9. http://www.forbes.com/sites/michaelzakkour/2014/04/30/copycat-china-still-a-problem-for-brands-chinas-future-just-ask-apple-hyatt-starbucks/
10. Example borrowed from Antifragile by Nassim Taleb

11. Peter Drucker (1974) Management: tasks, responsibilities, practices. p. 181. Source: http://bit.ly/1K8KvP4

12. Author Interview with Jesse Lawler. To listen to Jesse's interview, please visit taylorpearson.me/eoj

13. For further reading on how power distribution effects, see The Dictator's Handbook: http://www.amazon.com/The-Dictators-Handbook-Behavior-Politics/dp/1610391845

CHAPTER 2

14. http://www.washingtonpost.com/wp-dyn/content/article/2008/02/22/AR2008022202283_2.html?sid=ST2008022202336

15. http://www.nytimes.com/2015/04/19/opinion/sunday/the-machines-are-coming.html?smprod=nytcore-iphone&smid=nytcore-iphone-share&_r=1

16. http://www.wsj.com/articles/SB10001424053111903480904576512250915629460

17. http://www.cs.utexas.edu/~fussell/courses/cs352h/papers/moore.pdf

CHAPTER 3

18. http://portalseven.com/employment/unemployment_rate_u6.jsp

19. http://www.newyorkfed.org/research/current_issues/ci20-1.pdf

20. http://www.nytimes.com/2013/02/20/business/college-degree-required-by-increasing-number-of-companies.html?ref=business&_r=1&

21. http://www.nalp.org/uploads/Classof2013SelectedFindings.pdf

22. http://www.businessweek.com/articles/2012-06-12/mba-pay-peering-into-the-future

23. For a full explanation of the Framework from Dave Snowden, see https://www.youtube.com/watch?v=N7oz366X0-8

24. https://hbr.org/2007/11/a-leaders-framework-for-decision-making

SECTION 2

25. You'll note that these periods roughly follow Moore's Law, with each period halving the time of the previous one Agricultural (400 years), Industrial (200 years), Knowledge (100 years).

CHAPTER 4

26. http://www.oecd.org/edu/50495363.pdf

27. Author Interview with Andrew Youderian. To download the full interview on how Andrew left his investment banking job and started his business, go to http://taylorpearson.me/eoj/

SECTION 3

28. Daniel Kahneman, Thinking Fast and Slow, page 288-9

29. We also ignore how much upside there is. If you go talk to 10 girls and nine laugh and spit in your face and one turns into a deeply meaningful relationship that you spend years in and is emotionally satisfying, it's still a net positive by a wide margin. If you start 10 companies, lose $1000 on the first nine and make $1 million on the 10th, you're net positive even though you "failed" nine out of then times.

SECTION 4

30. To download the full interview with Derek Sivers about how he turned a side project, CD Baby, into a 75 person business and the qualities of musicians that are successful selling online (and how those lessons transfer to other industries), go to http://taylorpearson.me/eoj

31. To download an interview with Dan on how he turned a $40,000 per year web design agency Into a $40,000 per month recurring revenue service, go to http://taylorpearson.me/eoj

CHAPTER 8

32. Kevin Kelly, write about his the phenomenon in more detail at http://kk.org/thetechnium/2008/03/1000-true-fans/

33. To hear more from Andrew about the lifestyle and business possibilities enabled by the eCommerce drop shipping model and why individuals with hard skills and ambition has more opportunity than ever and why those without are screwed, download his interview at http://taylorpearson.me/eoj

34. http://www.innosight.com/innovation-resources/strategy-innovation/upload/creative-destruction-whips-through-corporate-america_final2012.pdf

CHAPTER 9

35. http://www.softwarebyrob.com/ and http://www.startupsfortherestofus.com/

36. To hear Rob's fully story of how he left his path towards CEO of a $500 million company to move into running his own business, download his interview at http://taylorpearson.me/eoj

37. You can learn more about Andrew and download a free guide he offers on starting a Dropshipping Business at ecommercefuel.com or you can go to taylorpearson.me/eoj to hear an intreview with Andrew about how he built his business.
38. You can learn more about Nathan and the strategies he uses for pricing and selling his ebooks at NathanBarry.com.
39. A productized service is a service where the delivery is standardized. Instead of having to deliver a custom project each time, the delivery is defined into a specific process making the business more scalable. You can download a series on getting started with Productized services at http://www.tropicalmba.com/podcasts/
40. You can learn more about John's story and how he built his business by dowloading an interview with him at taylorpearson.me/eoj.

CHAPTER 10

41. See Benjamin Franklin, An American Life
42. For more details on LinkedIn's approach to Apprenticeships, see: The Alliance - Ben Casnocha and Reid Hoffman
43. To download a version of this hiring process for your use, visit taylorpearson.me/eoj

SECTION 5

44. For a fuller treatment see Guns, Germs and Steel by Jared Diamond
45. Drucker, the Collected works of management
46. http://eh.net/encyclopedia/hours-of-work-in-u-s-history/
47. http://www.huffingtonpost.com/2014/07/17/map-happiness-benchmark_n_5592194.html

CHAPTER 11

48. DeMarco, MJ (2011-01-04). The Millionaire Fastlane: Crack the Code to Wealth and Live Rich for a Lifetime (p. 74). Viperion Publishing. Kindle Edition.
49. DeMarco, MJ (2011-01-04). The Millionaire Fastlane: Crack the Code to Wealth and Live Rich for a Lifetime (p. 83). Viperion Publishing. Kindle Edition.
50. http://www.perrymarshall.com/2100/tactical-triangle/

51. Sourced from http://foreverjobless.com/ev-millionaires-math/. For a full interview with Billy Murphy on how he built his businesses an further elaboration of Expected Value, visit http://taylorpearson.me/eoj

CHAPTER 12

52. Davison, Ron (2012-07-11). The Fourth Economy: Inventing Western Civilization (p. 346–347). Kindle Edition.
53. To hear a full interview with Dan about how his realization that middle class kids with second rate college degrees can get rich, the democratization of distribution, and decreasing manufacturing costs in China let him build his business while travelling the world, go to http://taylorpearson.me/eoj
54. Author Interview with Rob Walling. For the full interview and to download all the bonuses, go to http://taylorpearson.me/eoj

CHAPTER 13

55. Pink, Daniel H. (2011-04-05). Drive: The Surprising Truth About What Motivates Us (Kindle Locations 178-180). Penguin Group US. Kindle Edition.
56. Pink, Daniel H. (2011-04-05). Drive: The Surprising Truth About What Motivates Us (Kindle Locations 283-289). Penguin Group US. Kindle Edition.
57. Henry Sauerman and Wesley Cohen, "What Makes Them Tick? Employee Motives and Firm Innovation," NBER Working Paper No. 14443, October 2008.
58. Dan Ariely, Uri Gneezy, George Lowenstein, and Nina Mazar, "Large Stakes and Big Mistakes," Federal Reserve Bank of Boston Working Paper No. 05-11, July 23, 2005
59. Pink, Daniel H. (2011-04-05). Drive: The Surprising Truth About What Motivates Us
60. https://www.youtube.com/watch?v=6h5cY7d6nPU
61. http://www.inc.com/allison-fass/peter-thiel-mark-zuckerberg-luck-day-facebook-turned-down-billion-dollars.html
62. Pink, Daniel H. (2011-04-05). Drive: The Surprising Truth About What Motivates Us (Kindle Locations 1836-1848). Penguin Group US. Kindle Edition.

CONCLUSION

63. JFK's speech at Rice University on September 12th, 1962

64. Source: Peter Thiel, Zero to One

65. Author interview with Rob Walling, to download the full interview, go to http://taylorpearson.me/eoj

NEXT STEPS

66. http://articles.mercola.com/sites/articles/archive/2014/08/10/high-intensity-strength-training.aspx

67. Source: http://pmarchive.com/guide_to_career_planning_part1.html

Made in the USA
Lexington, KY
12 September 2015